Small Triumphs

Lessons in Alzheimer's and Love

Holly E. Stern

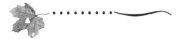

Trade Paperback ISBN: 979886 1926324

Printed in the United States of America

Design by Kim T. Griswell

10 9 8 7 6 5 4 3 2 1

First Edition

To Don, who taught me about unconditional love.

To my parents, who taught me the love of language.

To Ted, who teaches me every day the love and

support a big brother can give.

CONTENTS

FORWARD

This is the book I would have wanted to read while I followed the trajectory of Alzheimer's with my husband, Don. These are the stories, the lessons, the laughter, and the love that came out of those years. I have put them on paper, in the hope they might lighten the load for others.

If you are caring for someone with dementia, your experience may differ significantly from ours. The disease can lead you in many directions. But perhaps you will find in these pages some companionship along your path.

This is both a love story and an attempt to wrest some meaning from a cruel, senseless disease, as it slowly erased my husband over the last decade of his life. When dealing with dementia of any sort, including Alzheimer's, there are rarely major victories. But along the way, there may be a myriad of small triumphs. For me, focusing on those transformed my life.

The book is organized topically, rather than strictly chronologically. In addition to the narrative of our experience, I have inserted other writing I did at the time, both poetry and prose, following the relevant chapters. Occasionally, the same information reappears, as I digested it in different ways.

I have always loved language in its many forms. Words, along with music and friendship, became my life raft, while I plied the turbulence of caregiving and loss.

May this book help buoy you, as well.

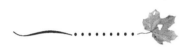

The Journey

In the Beginning

I remember when I first realized something was terribly wrong. It was November of 2011. We had been refurbishing our upstairs, repairing cracks in the plaster in our bedroom and office, texturing the walls, painting. Getting little sleep. All in an attempt to be ready for a scheduled carpet installation.

In keeping with the character of our 1926 house, we were texturing by hand with a sponge and joint compound. My husband, Don, who had taken early retirement years before, was doing most of the work. I helped out as time allowed, but I was still busy with my career as a professional violinist.

Don was the most generous, patient person I had ever met. He was truly one to go the extra mile. A lavish approach, however, is not a virtue when you are texturing a wall. If a little bit of joint compound is good, it does not follow that a LOT is even better. We had a regular cycle of Don applying texture, only to have to sand it down to a reasonable topography. His patience wore thin and his body wore out.

One night I painted away frantically in the office, while my husband got some much needed sleep. When he woke up to help me, he began doing bizarre things, like getting hinge grease on a freshly painted door and otherwise putting us further behind our deadline. Even accounting for the fact that he didn't ordinarily do well on little sleep, this behavior was alarming. Suddenly the odd occurrences that had been happening with increased frequency fell into place.

I knew then we were in trouble.

How had I not seen it coming? Don's mother and her father (whom I'd never met) had suffered from dementia of some sort. But my mother-in-law was in her 80s when it struck, and Don was only in his late 60s. And to be honest, my husband was less than exemplary when it came to focus and detail work. It suddenly hit me that what I had been observing lately—misplaced items, diminished logical thinking, decreased communication—was not a character flaw but an illness of the brain. The bedrock of my life began to crack.

Don must have felt it, too, because in the months that followed, I watched him sit on the couch and age before my eyes. Normally an active person, he developed neuropathy, pain which began in his feet and gradually crept up his legs. The doctors could find no cause for it. He was not diabetic, nor had he had any cancer treatments that could have triggered it. In fact, he was a very healthy person. Except that now he was in constant pain.

How much of it was physical and how much psychological? I never figured that out. I only know we tried many things to rid him of the pain: medications (from which he got only the side effects), nutrition, acupuncture, herbal remedies, chiropractic treatments, exercises, tapping. There is a theory that pain in the feet is an indication of a fear of moving forward, a fear of the future. In some ways, that made the most sense.

In the end, the neuropathy disappeared. When exactly, I don't know. I just realized one day that he'd stopped complaining about it. I didn't dare ask, because it had become such an identity for him: HE was a person who suffered from neuropathy. He told everyone who asked how he was doing, remarked about it constantly. Understandable for someone in chronic pain.

And then somehow, long after we'd stopped trying to fix the problem, it was gone. Vanished. He still had feeling in his feet, so it wasn't nerve die-off. Perhaps that part of his brain had ceased to make the connections necessary for a pain loop. Perhaps he was finally ready to step into the future.

As a performing musician and teacher, I have always been fascinated by how the brain works...or doesn't. How do we remember things? What do we need to think, at any given moment, to execute a task successfully? How do we make critical choices?

I began to realize Don's visual memory was no longer reliable. Items in the kitchen turned up in the wrong places. Recycling was tossed in the yard debris; garbage ended up in the recycling bin. I found myself asking, *Will anything ever work right again?* Sadly, the answer was no.

When you have been a successful team for decades, it is hard to reconcile that you can no longer delegate tasks. In my case, hope sprang eternal. Which is another way of saying I was slow to learn. I would try to give Don a simple task—set the table perhaps—only to discover that it, too, was beyond his grasp. In retrospect, it must have been very frustrating for him to feel like he was always failing at something he couldn't quite understand but thought he should. And as the responsibilities began to fall totally on my shoulders, I was not good at hiding my own frustrations.

Then came the most glaring example of lost visual memory, when he could no longer drive alone to places that were once very familiar. I can only imagine how scary that must have been for him. Where there had been an internal map, I suspect that now there was only a blank page. The word that kept coming to my mind was "untethered." Nothing to hang on to.

As his disease progressed, I took on several new roles. I became the Mother Duck, with Don imprinted on me for safety and direction. I joked about being his auxiliary hard drive, remembering what he could not. And in public, I was his interpreter, explaining the mysteries of a world that no longer made sense... calming him, while the developmental clock in his brain hit the reverse button.

BACK FROM THE BRINK

In my mind
I stand
Toes clenched around
The precipice
Arm tight around
One lone snag
Staring into
The abyss

Dread
Like a heavy overcoat
Tries to blanket
The panic
Hold it down
Steady it

And then he says,
"Can I make you a sandwich?"
And I ease myself back
From the brink
Inching my way to the
New normalcy
Grateful for a
Sandwich
Love made

A Man of Many Talents

One of the cruelest things about dementia is that it can steal your past, as well as your future. This is true not only for the people with the disease, but also for those who love them. The longer the illness, the harder it becomes to remember how they were when they were healthy.

So, as I write this chapter, it is not only to tell you about the man I loved deeply for over 32 years, but to attempt to break through the blankness caused by the stress of caregiving and the long slow path of grief.

Thankfully, as time distances me from his death, I am better able to remember the Don I knew before the disease took its toll. And I take great comfort that I have my journals, with daily entries that stretch back to before I met him. I have not lost him entirely.

For you to understand what happened to us, you need to know what was there before the Alzheimer's. Here is a bit about Don.

Often, when you want to describe someone, you begin with their profession. Don was well educated. He was "all but dissertation" for a PhD in psychology.

He'd assisted on research that led the fledgling copier industry to employ light waves that were less injurious to the user's eyes. The research was also important to the Department of Defense, and for this, his employer got him a critical deferment from the draft, just as Don was about to enlist. I shudder to think of what going to war would have done to this tenderhearted soul.

Don was a man of many talents, skilled at working with people and animals, as well as the machinery involved in various research projects. But research money comes and goes, and at various times he ventured into sales—life insurance, medical supplies, sailboats, cars, nutritional supplements. He did not, however, have the instincts of a salesperson. People loved to buy cars from him, because he got them excellent deals, but it meant that some months he brought home only minimum wage.

When I met him, just shy of his 44th birthday, he had more or less found his niche helping people who were impaired in one way or another. He'd worked with developmentally delayed adults and people with head injuries, and for the last 5 1/2 years of employment, he was a service coordinator for adults with chronic mental illness. He had a knack for understanding and connecting with people. His clients and coworkers loved him, and he took great pride in making their lives more comfortable.

Eventually, however, burnout set in. When the agency he worked for needed to restructure, requiring him to take an even heavier client load, it seemed wiser to resign. I, meanwhile, was at my busiest, between performing and teaching, and we were trying to co-author a mystery novel, so having a house spouse made a lot of sense. To the envy of many, Don retired at the age of 51.

Fortunately, Don was not defined by his profession. Instead, as perhaps it always should be, he was the sum of his character traits: kindness, generosity, a desire to help people, intelligence, patience, a great sense of humor, creativity, a willingness to try new things. He was an optimist, and John Lennon's "Imagine" was his favorite song. He lived life with an open heart, often crying over some news story as if it were his own. A hard worker, he gave his all to any job he undertook. And most important to me, he was a sweet and loving man.

To many, retirement is a huge adjustment. Often people are at a loss when they are suddenly home all day. But somehow, Don never seemed bored. He loved to read, and to write poetry and short stories, and there was our mystery novel to work on. He was the plot guy; I was the wordsmith. And he was the person who made my busy life possible.

About the time Don retired, someone shared with us America's 1950s rules for being a good housewife—instructions on having the children cleaned up and quiet for the husband's return to his castle, refreshing your make-up, having something delicious cooking on the stove. Don's daughter was not living with us, so there were no kids to subdue. But one day, early in his retirement, I walked in the back door after a long day of rehearsals, to find my husband stirring a pot on the stove, rouge on his cheeks, a bow in his hair, and a smile of domestic bliss on his face. A sight I wish every woman could experience. I don't remember the instructions saying you were to make your spouse

The perfect housewife

laugh, but it was definitely what I needed.

Looking back, I'm struck by how much self-confidence Don had. He took on new challenges with a fearlessness I could only envy. Let me share a few examples.

Not long after he retired, the non-profit he'd worked for asked him to be on their board of directors. The agency was originally started by parents of adults with chronic mental illness. Don was able to add the perspective of the staff on the front lines. While he was on the board, they managed to build HUD housing for some of their clients and to find a good replacement for the retiring executive director. Don was board president when the agency merged with another. It always amazed me that he was able to maneuver these procedures, with all their legal ramifications, and that he knew how to run a tight meeting, in which

A dream fulfilled

everyone felt heard. Where did he learn that?

His fearlessness surfaced when a close friend took him on an airplane ride in a Cessna 150. My husband was smitten! Flying was something he'd dreamt of since he was a child, and, though it scared me to have him up there in a little one-engine plane, I could not easily dismiss such passion. He proved himself a capable pilot and even learned to fly taildraggers, like the ones used in WWII, which was another key interest of his. On a few occasions, I screwed up my courage and accompanied him. It was easy to see why he loved it so much.

Then one Sunday, while I was out of town, Don went to church and heard a 14-year-old congregant play Camille Saint-Saëns' "The Swan" on the cello. My husband sat there and told himself, *I may never be as good as this young man, but I could learn to play the cello.* In high school, Don had played the sousaphone, and he loved the sound of the

Christmas duets

lower instruments. So when he picked me up at the airport a couple of days later, he announced we now had a rented cello in the house. He was almost 62 at that point. For a few years I was the note-taking "mom" at his lessons, as two of our friends, both cellists in the Oregon Symphony, agreed (in succession) to teach him. Don was an earnest learner, and I have some very dear photos of him playing Christmas carols for the family.

Don's many friends remember him for his kindness and generosity. He would have made a great philanthropist, had he been rich. The one time he got a windfall (a few thousand in inheritance from an uncle), he had it doled out in no time, to a friend in need and to various non-profits. When we would discuss how much to give for our joint charitable donations, Don would often advocate doubling what I had already considered a liberal amount. It was up to me to find the sweet spot, a necessity of my being in a low paid profession.

But generosity is not defined by money alone. For years, Don would begin each morning praying for people he knew. There might be as many as 25 or 30, and I wondered how he kept track of them all and what he prayed for. It was his way of putting positive energy out into the Universe, of showing his love, of being as helpful as he could.

If you asked Don for a favor, chances were very good he would do it. Or even if you didn't ask. Once, a friend of ours (not someone we knew well at the time) needed to get to Eugene, 110 miles away from our home in Portland, Oregon. Perhaps he was asking to borrow money for bus fare. Without another thought, Don said he'd fly him there. Many years later, when I was making short videos of greetings to bring Don while he was in foster care, this man recounted how much that trip—and the extra $50—meant to him. This was but one of many kindnesses Don bestowed on the world. He gave easily and never counted the cost.

A Love Story

I often wonder if there's a Department of Holly somewhere, orchestrating my life. I could just imagine a bunch of workers running around, putting things in place. If I remember to pause long enough to look, the result of their handiwork is stunning.

Shortly after my 38th birthday, on a drive with my brother, I suddenly blurted out, "I feel like I'm about to meet someone important." Where did that come from? The words left my mouth with neither plan nor preamble, as if someone else had commandeered my brain.

Less than a month later, Don, quite literally, walked into my life.

There was something magical about the way we met. I first saw Don on the second Sunday of September, 1987, when he held open the door of the First Unitarian Church for me. Tall, with striking blue eyes and a kindly expression, he caught my attention, but try as I might, there was no chance to meet him at the coffee hour after the service. He seemed to know a lot of people, and I wondered why I'd never seen him before.

The following Friday, I was performing with the Portland Baroque Orchestra. As I looked out at the audience, I thought, *This is a great bunch of music lovers. Surely there must be people out there for us single women.* Unbeknownst to me, Don was not only in the audience, he was the sole person to fill out a form to volunteer for the orchestra.

But still we did not meet.

And we almost didn't meet two days later, on Sunday. I hung around the coffee hour after church, hoping he would miraculously stop talking to all those other people, while I passed the time conversing with someone else.

Finally, I gave up and went to another part of the church for the initial meeting of a social group. It was not a singles group, per se, and I figured I'd at least meet some interesting people. Several minutes later, who should walk in but Don.

Now, there are two versions of the story, but only mine is correct. Don would say I was wearing a red dress and I was smiling at him, patting the empty chair beside me. I *was* wearing a red dress, and there *was* an empty chair beside me, and most likely I *was* smiling at him. But I did NOT pat the chair. Just for the record.

After the meeting, we chatted. "And what do you do?" Don asked.

When I told him I was a musician, his eyes lit up. "Oh, I heard a great concert Friday night. The Portland Baroque Orchestra."

"Then you heard me play," I replied.

We had lunch together, exchanging tidbits of our lives. I loved that I could get him to laugh, and as I looked into his amazing blue eyes, I thought, *Those eyes have not laughed enough recently.* Don't ask me where I got the idea; I haven't the foggiest.

THEN we discovered that neither of us had been hiking much over the summer. And here it was, September 20th, so we exchanged phone numbers and....

He called the next day. He had Wednesday free. Did I want to go for a hike with him? As it turned out, I, too, had Wednesday free. I offered to make lunch for us. To which he responded, "Then I'll make dinner." You see why I fell in love with him?

Our first date, which happened to be on the autumnal equinox, was a hike to Mirror Lake and on up to the top of Tom, Dick, Harry Mountain, about 50 miles east of Portland. At the summit, we found a huge

View from Beanbag Rock

boulder, somewhat hollowed out, and crawled up on it to eat our lunch with a magnificent view of Mt. Hood. Over the years, we made that hike many times, always happy to seat ourselves in Beanbag Rock, as we dubbed it, with its stunning panorama.

In the car, on our way to and from the hike, I got to know more about him. He had left his marriage of 23 years several months earlier (that would explain the eyes that hadn't laughed enough recently) and had a 13-year-old daughter. I was impressed that he said nothing negative about his wife, with whom, it turned out, I had done several performances, playing in orchestras while she sang. It was nice to learn he was used to the care and feeding of a musician.

That was Wednesday. Thursday evening, he came to the dress rehearsal of the opera I was performing. I must have seen him on Friday (though there are no details in my journal), because for Saturday, I wrote, "A day without Don...almost. He was certainly there in my thoughts...and later in a note on my windshield after the opera." A sweet surprise.

By Sunday, we had more inside jokes than I've ever had with anyone. And that was just the first week! As it turned out, in 11 weeks, we only missed seeing each other six days, and three of them were in that initial week. Knowing the pitfalls of rebound romances, we were going "full speed ahead with the brakes on." But I was not rebounding from anything, and I was trying to be very clear-headed about this new man in my life.

One thing that impressed me early on was to find

that, in addition to being able to cook, he knew how to keep a clean apartment. I noted with surprise that he could use my bathroom and leave it with no trace he'd been there. I promised myself to thank his mother, if and when I should meet her.

At the 2 1/2 week mark, Don came to Portland Baroque Orchestra's traditional Thursday night spaghetti dinner, after which we musicians split up to rehearse chamber music for our upcoming trip to Timberline Lodge on Mt. Hood. Apparently, Don fit right in with my friends, because several of them encouraged me to bring him with me for the weekend. There was plenty of room in the men's dorm, they said, and no one counted noses on the meals we were provided.

Remember Don's offering to volunteer for Portland Baroque Orchestra two days before we met? That weekend at Timberline Lodge, he made himself extremely useful, helping to carry the harpsichord and hawking CDs to benefit the orchestra. After which, he got the PBO Seal of Approval. He was one of us.

It amazed me how gregarious he was. He was so good with people, even strangers. When I learned that he'd been Senior Class President in high school, I quipped that I was dating the second most popular guy in the Universe (THE most popular being, obviously, the Student Body President). This was heady stuff for someone shy like me. At every high school reunion we attended over the years, it was obvious his classmates adored him. At 6'6" tall, he was easy to pick out in a crowd, and they flocked to him.

But he was not a jock. His popularity came from his kindness and warmth and sense of humor. He told me about his senior prom, to which he had planned to take his steady girlfriend. There was another girl, however, who did not have a date, so Don asked his steady if she would mind if he took the other girl to the prom for the first hour. How many 18-year-old guys would think to do that? How many steady girlfriends would agree it was a good idea?

So this was the man I had fallen in love with.

It was uncanny how similar our tastes were—in food, in entertainment, in hobbies, in humor. After we had known each other about a year, we made a wonderful discovery. On a camping trip at a friend's farm, we took turns reading to each other from a mystery novel I'd been given. I will never forget how delicious that felt, to be read to by flashlight, with the creek murmuring in the background. From then on, sharing books (especially mysteries) was our favorite form of entertainment. If I were baking, it was a joy to listen to the story unfolding. At night, I would read, as he rubbed on my sore muscles. And in the morning, we could discuss who we thought "dunnit."

I later found that, if I really needed a nap in preparation for a performance but could not get to sleep, having Don read to me kept me dozing as long as the story continued. If he stopped, I woke up. Many a time he read for an hour or more, just so I could get my rest. And then, of course, I'd have to read it all again later, having slept through dozens of pages.

There are few things that test a couple's compatibility more than house projects. When we bought our home in 1989, it was like taking possession of a handsome being that had been forced to wear a Halloween costume since the 1970s. Previous owners had installed external grade T-111 siding (the stuff with brown plastic knotholes) as paneling in the living and dining rooms. They were so proud of it, they signed their great achievement underneath. I added to their message, "And in 1989, Don and Holly remedied the situation." Then we covered it with drywall.

The "paneling" also hid a set of three windows on the north wall of the dining room. Z-BRICK concealed the original yellow tiles around the fireplace. The kitchen sported crumbling fake parquet linoleum and tiled counters that looked like Attila the Hun had visited. Throughout, to add to the "coziness," lovely wood floors slumbered under flea-infested, dog-stained brown shag carpet.

But the house had good bones and a backyard with space for a garden, and we loved the neighborhood. So we got to work. The next many years were shrouded in construction dust. Happily, we proved remodeling was one more area in which we were well suited, despite our different backgrounds. Don had a fair amount of experience with houses; I had none. What I brought to the table was a logical and inquiring mind. We soon found that, with our different perspectives, projects done together were much more successful than if we'd attempted them alone.

Now, when I look around the house on the anniversary of our move-in date, I have to struggle to find anything we did not redo. Those renovations speak to my husband's talents, as well as our ability to work together.

Don proved to be handy not only at house projects, but also at cleaning. And he enjoyed it! I did not and was happy to relinquish this role. I used to joke that it was a spoiled woman who did not know how to turn on her own vacuum cleaner. Sadly, as Don's dementia set in, I had to figure it out, but God bless my husband for all those years I was pampered. And yes, the day I was introduced to Don's mother, I did indeed thank her for raising such an extraordinary man.

When I met Don, he had not traveled farther abroad than Canada and Mexico. I, on the other hand, had made it around the world before I turned six. Thanks to my cultural anthropologist father, I had lived in foreign countries for two years of my life: in Rangoon, Burma (now Myanmar), at the age of five; and in The Hague, The Netherlands, at the age of 15. When I was 28, I lived in Puerto Rico for a year, while I played in their symphony orchestra. And there had been shorter trips abroad, to Europe and to Chile.

So when we finally got around to marrying, about six years into our relationship, it seemed a good idea to take my husband traveling for our honeymoon. I dusted off my Dutch and French languages, and we spent a week in The Netherlands and a week in Paris and surrounding areas. Knowing from past experience that traveling can sometimes reveal undiscovered traits in your partner (and not always happy ones), I did not know what to expect. With Don, however, you might have thought we'd been at it for ages, companionable globetrotters that we were.

Over the years, we made it to Europe several times, as well as to Thailand, Bali, and Brazil. Don dubbed me his "tour guide," and for the most part, we traveled on our own, with a flexible itinerary. One of my sweetest memories was of a Mother's Day in southern France. While I slept in, Don set out to find pastries to bring me. Armed with a scant French vocabulary, he went about accosting the natives with a hopeful, "Patisserie?" He returned triumphant, proud of his accomplishment and bearing the most delicious breakfast a person could wish for. My hero!

I once contemplated what my life would have been like had I not met Don. The fact that we adored one another gave me the confidence to try new things, to experiment and explore, knowing he would always be there for me. For all of our 32 years together, we still lit up when we spotted each other across a room filled with people. Even at the end, when it was only the two of us, and I had just come through the doorway at his foster care home, entering as a stranger until recognition brought a smile to his face—even then, there was magic.

My homemade
cake stayed
upright!

Still celebrating...21 years later

PUN-ISHMENT

It was too good to wait
Till morning
Puns are not meant
To be wasted

I nudged you awake

"What does a philanthropist
Wear on his head?"

Silence

I could wait no longer
"A distributor cap!"

Years of doing tune-ups
On my 1976 Corolla
Had taught me this
This pun
Waiting
To happen

Months later
The gift
Boxed and wrapped

Under the tree
My very own
(Paper)
Distributor cap

The tag says
"One size fits all philanthropists"
At the top of the cap
An "In" portal
On the sides
Four connectors:
"Homeless Waifs"
"Endangered Stuff (Animals, Arts Groups, etc.)"
"Flora, Air, Water, etc."
"Lesser Weevils (Politics)"
(As in "the lesser of two evils"
You had your own puns)
And finally, on the cap's bill:
"You owe $ $ $"

We had always had this
This connection
Humor understood
Shared

We always had this

                    Until we didn't

This is who we were

Into the Wilderness

W e had 24 years of amazing companionship... equals, contributing to and completing each other...until Alzheimer's came, first stealing parts so small I could convince myself they were not really gone, only temporarily misplaced...until the thief became emboldened and I could no longer ignore the empty spaces left behind.

I remember reading that Alzheimer's disease can go undetected for decades before manifesting itself. It's a sneaky swindler, and those of us who are "of an age" often find ourselves questioning if a forgotten name or word is the first step down a slippery slope. How do you separate character traits and normal aging from the progression of Alzheimer's or other forms of dementia?

At this time, Alzheimer's can be definitively diagnosed only through an autopsy. But I've heard one indication of dementia is when you no longer remember how to perform daily acts of living, like feeding yourself. So give yourself a break the next time your friend's name is suddenly nowhere to be found. Laugh and move on.

Sadly, Don's "missing pieces" were not so benign.

In the end, Don's brain autopsy did come back positive for Alzheimer's disease, and at the most severe degree. Somehow, I found it comforting to know I had not imagined what was happening and that there really was nothing more I could have done to change the trajectory of his decline.

So what did the thief steal? In general, the handholds that allowed Don to function: his sense of identity, his ability to respond appropriately to situations, his memories of how things worked. Eventually, even the words to communicate what he was experiencing. But these things eroded over time, sometimes so subtly that they went unnoticed, until one day I realized they had all but vanished.

In retrospect, I now recognize that Don's increasing need to talk about himself was probably an attempt to hold on to an identity that was slipping away. Old stories, retold when we gathered with friends—and separately to me, as if I hadn't already heard them many times over—were also a safe way to interact. He could contribute to the conversation without having to form new ideas.

He continued to enjoy reading, including tomes of such depth I would have been hard pressed to follow the ideas put forth. But by then the very act of reading, the sequence of words no matter what their meaning, probably made him feel that his brain was still functioning somewhat normally.

As the disease progressed, he became more literal in his interpretations, and he would often comment in the margins of books whose subtleties now eluded him. A paperback copy of Ogden Nash's *A Penny Saved Is Impossible*, a book whose humor Don enjoyed in earlier years, shows evidence of his outrage. "That's STUPID!!!" was penned heavily onto the cover, with squiggles to obliterate Mr. Nash.

As for his early morning prayers, they had long since ceased. He claimed not to believe in God. It was not said with rancor, but rather as if he felt an Intelligent Man would not fall for such things, and at that point, he needed to retain that image of himself. Faith was one more thing the thief had stolen.

There was another behavior I did not immediately fit into the puzzle. When we were planning a trip out of town, Don would look forward to it for weeks. "How long till we go to L.A.?" he might ask. And I would tell him, beginning the countdown to The Day. But the morning after we arrived at our destination, he would wake up and say, "Are we going home today?" It felt like he had a leash to home base and he needed to make sure it held.

Watching the regression was like seeing the wheels of Don's life come off, lug nut by lug nut. In healthier times, we had a tradition for the nights I had a pre-concert rehearsal before a performance. I would carpool with a friend, and Don would show up at the break after the rehearsal with dinner he'd either made or gotten as take-out.

Then things became unpredictable. Either the meal would have no source of protein (I burn through food fast when I'm performing) or he would have bought enough for only one person or he would have forgotten to pay the parking meter. I tried to amuse myself by wondering what would go wrong THIS time, but in truth it was not funny.

I've been asked if Don was aware of what was happening to him.

There was one morning he woke me up with, "I am going to stay with you as long as I can." When I asked him about it, he had no memory of having said it. Perhaps I misheard. Or was this a brief moment of lucidity?

I kept listening for something, anything that would let me know he wanted to discuss his mental decline, but it came up clearly only once. He was going through an uncharacteristic period of depression, and one night I found he'd left our bed and was sleeping on the couch. I asked what was wrong.

"I'm dying," he said.

"Your body is very healthy," I replied.

"But my brain is dead."

My heart broke for him. "I'll take care of you," I said. "We'll get through this together."

It was about this same period that he took off his wedding ring and said, "Find someone else to use this." I immediately returned it to him and only agreed to keep it for him when he moved into foster care.

So on one level, he knew. Maybe I should have

brought the subject up, to give him more of an opening. It's tricky: how much would the truth have helped him, and how much would it have further devastated him? When our financial advisor broached it with him, Don seemed unaware of (or unwilling to admit to) the seriousness of the deterioration.

In retrospect, perhaps I could have said, "I know things are a bit rough for you right now. Do you want to talk about it?" But by then, that may have been too many words for him to sort out.

If you are dealing with someone who is still in the early stages of dementia, be sure to watch for opportunities to discuss what they are going through. They may be aching for someone to hear what they're experiencing. They may need your reassurance. Dementia can be a scary and lonely place.

How do you live in a world you do not understand? It must be extremely terrifying when old landmarks no longer look familiar, when any sort of logic is hard won and fleeting, when there is nothing to hold on to.

This was where Alzheimer's led us. Fear took over Don's life and transformed my peaceful husband into a combative man. Thankfully, we found a way to retrieve his sweet personality. Other things were lost for good.

The Fear Factor

As Don's capacity to process information diminished, the world became increasingly unfathomable to him. Eventually I learned that if his behavior didn't make sense, it was probably rooted in fear.

Take walking through the neighborhood, for instance. This was something we'd always loved to do. When he was younger and still 6'6" (a foot-and-a-half taller than I), I would walk fast and occasionally supplement with a few running steps to catch up. I suppose there was a time when we were pretty evenly matched, but the next thing I knew, he kept his pace two or three feet behind me. If I slowed down, he slowed down. If I sped up, he put on a bit of steam. I was constantly having to turn around, to make sure he was still there. He outweighed me by 60 pounds, so dragging him was not an option. (I know. I tried.)

Walks were no longer enjoyable, and I couldn't figure out why he wasn't keeping up. Now I realize he was probably just afraid I'd disappear and he'd get lost. He stayed where he had a good view of his Mother Duck. Interestingly, the few times we went to the coast and walked on the beach, he remained by my side. Why that was different, I don't know.

In the end, the fear was undeniable. I would try to walk him around the block, but when we got to the edge of our property, he would freeze. "We can't go there," he'd say. "We don't know those people." I would reassure him that we knew those neighbors and the ones who came next and the ones beyond them, and that besides, it was a public sidewalk. But he would go no farther. All we could do was turn around and go home.

When we were out in public, I had to keep a close eye on him. Strangers talking to him in a store—even just friendly banter—became alarming. To avoid a confrontation, I would step back out of Don's sight, look at the other person, and gently tap my temple, to indicate Don did not understand. That usually took care of the situation.

Inappropriate responses sometimes happened at church, too. If I had to go early to rehearse with the choir, Don would sit alone in the sanctuary and, I think in his mind, protect his territory. On more than one occasion, I had to make a beeline to soothe the person who had been told to "GET OUT!" But you know? All it took was one word of explanation—dementia—and compassion took the place of anger. Again, I did this away from Don, so he would not feel diminished.

At home, fear sometimes manifested itself in weird ways. At one point, Don became fixated on photographs of people in books. The person would then become real to him. On several occasions, Don told me we couldn't go into a particular room, because "that person" was in there. This was problematic when the book was open by the bed. I would tell him it was a picture, not a real person, but that made no difference. So I did the only thing I could think of. I picked up the book and closed it. "There," I said. "Now we can go to sleep." Lest you think me heartless, I did close the book gently, no matter how irritated I was. And Don seemed all right with that. We were in a world of extended reality.

Fishwifing

Let me not give the impression that I was always one of those cheerful, unflappable caregivers who knew instinctively what to do and discharged my duties seamlessly. In truth, I was way above my pay grade and extremely frustrated that I was becoming increasingly mired in something with no hope of success. I felt life closing in on me.

I still loved my husband very much. In that, I was extremely lucky. And most of the time, I could calmly look after him. But when it came to trying to give him a shower, no fishwife could outshout me. This was not a helpful tactic, I hasten to say.

As one geriatric psychiatrist pointed out, we are taught all our lives not to take our clothes off in front of strangers. And then dementia hits, and that is exactly what we are asked to do. Even after 30 years together, I had become a stranger in this regard. Don's response to this intrusion on his body was to lash out. I learned to position myself in such a way that, if he shoved me, I would not get seriously hurt.

I remember one particular day when Don had

three layers of clothing on top and three layers on the bottom, and it was taking me 20 minutes to coax just one item off him. I felt I would grow old before I got him showered that day.

I considered hiring someone to bathe him, but "logic" told me he was even less apt to acquiesce to a stranger who hadn't lived with him for three decades. Now, in retrospect, I wonder if I'd overlooked the fact that professional caregivers are trained; I was not. I did find some help online in "Bathing Without a Battle."

Dementia is cruel in many ways, not the least of which is that you have the disconnect of being with someone who looks like an adult but often acts like a young child. I can't count the number of times I would give "helpful guidance," knowing full well there was no way Don would remember anything I said. Not that I let that stop me.

When Don got stuck in the Terrible Twos, I was beside myself. This was my sweet husband. How could this be happening? It was so out of character, that when he first tried to swear, he'd yell, "Go to heck!" He soon hit his stride with cursing, though it rarely went beyond "Damn it!!!"

I found myself having to keep close watch over my own mouth when we were out. Sometimes my irritation would bubble over and I was suddenly able to understand the mother whose toddler was misbehaving in public. It was a humbling experience. A fellow caregiver pointed out that it's the disease we're angry at, not the person, but to tell you the truth, that can be hard to remember when you're feeling exasperated.

Life moves slowly in the world of dementia. I was used to powering along at high speed. It took me quite a while to realize I needed to factor in a LOT more time to do everything. I felt like I was walking through molasses. And the worst part of it was that, at the end of the day, I had only accomplished the most mundane of tasks—cooking, cleaning, keeping my husband safe. An unrelenting wheel of drudgery. Never having raised kids of my own, this was new and daunting territory for me, and there wasn't any hope of the situation improving, as when a child grows up and learns new skills.

In addition, caregiving for someone with dementia is different from caregiving for someone who is physically ill. Dementia often destroys the ability to communicate verbally, which leaves both parties befuddled and frustrated. It also removes the sense of satisfaction that comes from words of appreciation for all your labors. Where was the man who responded to me in meaningful ways? We had entered our own private Hell, from which I needed to find an exit, if even for a brief time.

Then I discovered respite day care. It was offered one afternoon a week at a senior center for 3 1/2 hours. A good friend lived nearby, and most weeks she would fix me lunch and let me talk. Then we would cap it off by playing a Mozart violin duet, and I would return to pick up Don, refreshed. That became my island of sanity.

A few months later, I found another facility that offered several hours of respite care for as many as five days a week! I thought I'd died and gone to Heaven. Even a couple of extra days promised much needed breathing room for me and social interaction for Don. But it was not to be. In less than two weeks, he'd flunked that respite care. He'd misinterpreted what one of the staff was trying to do and had gotten angry. He still cut an imposing figure, so even a brief outburst was threatening.

It was then I realized I had to get Don's fearfulness under control. CBD oil calmed him somewhat, but only for a few hours. While I am not usually a fan of medications, it was obvious Don needed something more. A friend whose mother had done a complete 180 when they figured out the right combination of drugs encouraged me to seek medical advice. I took Don to a geriatric psychiatrist. Unless we got a handle on Don's anxiety, our options for his care were going to be a lot more limited, to say nothing of his enjoyment of life.

For those of you who go this route, be patient. People react differently to medications. It took a lot of experimentation, both with choosing the right combination of pharmaceutical drugs and adjusting the dosage. We were still tinkering when I moved Don into foster care, but fortunately the owner of the facility had far more experience than I and was able to work things out by consulting with the psychiatrist's nurse.

In the end, my husband's sweet nature resurfaced, much to my eternal gratitude.

There's No Place Like Home?

In the fall of 2017, I began hiring a caregiver to come to our home and be with Don for a couple of hours a week. This provided Don some stimulation from a professional who actually knew what she was doing, and I was able to escape briefly. But over the next six months, even with our caregiver and the once-a-week respite day care, Don continued to withdraw. Eventually, he was cocooning in bed. It took a supreme effort for anyone to coax him out.

A close and knowledgeable friend had been asking, "How will you know it's time?"

I replied, "When the physical care gets beyond me," thinking it might happen in a year or two.

In fact, that point had arrived without my realizing it. Within one 24-hour period, three people close to our situation independently voiced the opinion that it was time to move Don.

The truth came crashing down on me.

Some people try to keep their loved one at home as long as possible, but even if I'd hired around-the-clock care for Don, he still would have been isolated. And I would have felt trapped in my own house, trying to accommodate not only my husband, but various caregivers.

Fortunately, we had options. Many years earlier, when we had no clue what was around the corner, our financial advisor had recommended we get long term care insurance. While this industry has changed a lot since we got our policy, it is still worth looking into.

Nonetheless, hard as it had become to take care of Don, moving him seemed insurmountable, like a huge mountain I needed to scale. How do you take someone out of their home of almost three decades, knowing they are not coming back, distancing them from the one person who represents their security? There is no easy way to do this.

My knowledgeable (and generous!) friend and I began making the rounds of facilities. I was grateful she was experienced in this, because it can be very difficult comparing costs and services from one residence to another. We engaged an agency that finds places with openings and sets up appointments. This service is usually free to those who are looking; payment comes from the residence when a person moves in.

Don was not a wanderer, so we did not need a lockdown building or official memory care. The larger facilities offered some group activities, which I hoped might bring him out of his seclusion, but they also had a high rate of staff turnover and a lot of regulations and fees. And the rooms were unfurnished, meaning there were sizable costs and effort upfront, before you even knew if it was going to be a good fit. We looked at ten such places and had narrowed it down to a top candidate.

Then I took Don on an outing to a "memory cafe." This was something like a singalong with snacks. As we sat there, I realized how much he had declined since we had last attended two months previously. He wasn't connecting with the entertainment at all. Why, then, was I considering putting him in a larger facility? The lightbulb went on with blinding impact. A residential complex was not the right place for him. He would be lost in such an institution.

The next day, my friend and I began visiting adult foster care homes. That had been my original thought, until I got waylaid with the prospect of involving Don in group activities. In Oregon, adult care homes (which I also refer to as "foster care") can have a maximum of five residents. Many of them are owned by Romanian families, which, I was to discover, is a natural occupation for a culture raised to take care of their elders.

We saw a wide variety of homes. In general, they offered each resident their own furnished room, with some sort of communal dining area, and they cost less than the larger facilities. What appealed to us most was the feeling that clients were treated as part of the family.

It was at this point I realized that Don could actually

be happier in this setting than he was at home. I cannot begin to tell you what a comfort that thought was for me. We talk about aging in place, as if it were the ideal. For some, staying at home might be the perfect solution. For us, it was not.

But there was still that mountain to climb.

We found a gorgeous place for Don, and the owners came to our house to interview him. Not that he said much, because by then he was mostly non-verbal, but they liked him. All was set, except a date. As they asked when I wanted to move him, I found I could only choke back tears. I promised to call them.

The next day, I finally wrapped my mind around a schedule. But when I phoned the following morning, I discovered someone had appeared on their doorstep in crisis, cash in hand, and there went Don's new home.

I crumbled. I was emotionally exhausted and could not fathom more searching. Why was this happening? Didn't the Universe know I needed a break here? I lay on the grass and looked up at the spring sky, my heart aching.

And then it occurred to me. I had been working on a piece for a writers competition, about trust and faith. How could I submit it, if I didn't have faith that things would turn out as they were meant to, if I didn't trust there might be an even better solution for Don?

So the next day my amazingly generous friend and I were back at it, feeling dissatisfied with what we were seeing, because nothing measured up to the place I'd set my heart on. We'd gotten through our list for the day, when I pulled out another list I'd been given. Was there something else we could look at that was nearby? I poked an address into my phone and saw it was a three-minute walk from where we were. We drove around the corner and found the owners in the driveway.

They didn't have a vacancy but were willing to show us how they were set up. It gave us hope. Even more so, when the owner called her sisters, both of whom had foster homes, and discovered one of them had a vacancy at her residence. As we drove there, I realized this was where another friend had placed her husband. She'd told me she was very pleased with the care he was receiving.

It felt bright and fresh and friendly. We were impressed with the cleanliness. The live-in caregiver spoke warmly about the family members, who were not home at that moment. Shaped like an L, the house had one wing for the family and one for the five residents. The available room was sunny and looked out on a big deck, which joined the two sections of the house. As a bonus, the owners had three little boys, built-in entertainment for Don. We returned later, to meet the family and set up a time for an interview. A few days later, the owner came to see Don, and we agreed on a moving date.

I don't know how aware my husband was of what my friend and I had been doing during my frequent absences. Each time I left, I would put a note by his place at the dining room table, telling him I had gone to run errands and when I would be back. The notes gave him the sense of security he needed. PBS Kids television programs kept him company, and I let my neighbor know I was going out.

I tried to gently break the idea of moving to Don. There seemed to be two schools of thought about this. One said don't lie; the other recommended saying whatever was needed to smooth the departure. I aimed for something in between, mentioning that I had to have more help taking care of him. He seemed okay with that, whatever it translated to in his brain. Since time had little meaning for him at that point, I had this conversation the night before the move. I didn't want him stewing about some fearful future for any longer than needed.

But the next morning, he would not get out of bed. I explained we'd been invited to lunch with our new friend. He would not budge. Finally, I went out to the yard, picked a bouquet of foxgloves, and put them in a vase. Don loved flowers. I told him we were bringing them to our friends and that I needed him to hold them in the car, so they didn't tip over. Thus my beloved, helpful husband walked out of his home, so he could help me transport a bouquet of flowers.

While he had lunch, I scurried back to the house and gathered up the few things he'd need, plus some personal items to make his room look more like home. I remember seeing the empty pillowcase after I removed his pillow, thinking how much it looked like the sleeve over an amputated arm. That was how this whole removal felt—like I was having part of my body severed.

As with the advice on what to say about moving, the protocol for how to leave your spouse was also divided. Many places had a strict rule that I should not stay with him for the first night or two. Some even forbade visits for up to a week. This was supposed to remove any confusion about the fact that he was going to live there without me. To me that felt cruel. What was he going to think, when he woke in the middle of the night, in a strange place, without his Mother Duck to explain what was going on?

The other school of thought was more flexible, and some places even said I could sleep there for a couple of days. Our place at first acquiesced to my suggestion I spend the first night with Don. After getting him settled in, I wrote him a note, saying these nice people were going to take good care of him and that I'd be back. Then I left him and went straight to a friend's birthday party.

"Where's Don?" they greeted me. I immediately dissolved into a flood of tears. It was a fairly large gathering of people who knew us well, and it took until the fourth such question that I could explain without coming unglued. Practice does indeed help. While I do not recommend this as exemplary party behavior, the love and support of friends was exactly what I needed, and fortunately these were very good friends.

From there, I went to choir practice at our church.

Again, I was embraced with tenderness. I was going to need a lot of that in the coming days. I left, planning to stop by the house on my way to spend the night with Don.

But when I checked my texts, I was told he was fine, that I was not needed. So I left them to do what I'd hired them for: take care of my husband. And though I later learned he'd asked repeatedly, "Where's Holly?", he did indeed survive. I visited him daily, and by the third day, he looked around his room and said, "This is a nice place." To which my heart said a silent Hallelujah.

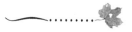

RELEASE

Touch the wound gently
And release

The empty chair
The mug no longer fragrant with herb tea

Touch but do not linger
Release

Practice telling
Till the words no longer drown
As they cross your lips

Nibble on grief

Release

RENT TO RENT

Merriam-Webster's Collegiate Dictionary, Eleventh Edition:

"**rent** *past and past part of* REND"
"**rend** ... *vb* ... **2** : to split or tear apart ... by violence"
"**rent** *n* ... **2** : a split in a party or organized group"

I don't know if you'd call my husband and me an "organized group." Organization wasn't one of our strong suits. But we were lucky. For most of our 31 years together, life was good. As close to a party as our busy schedules would permit.

That is, until my husband's Alzheimer's disease rent our lives, tearing our memories, and our dreams, into shreds and casting them to the winds like so many pieces of confetti.

Over the years, caregiving became increasingly difficult, until the day came when those close to me said, "It's time."

How do you remove someone from his home of 29 years, someone for whom you have become his anchor? There is no kind and gentle way to do this. It felt like a physical, violent tearing apart. A rent. And yet so necessary for both of us—he for better care, me to regain my life.

We are on the other side now. For the first time in almost eight months, he came home yesterday to celebrate a delayed Christmas with his family. It was magical. His laughter once again warmed the room. His smiles brightened our spirits.

And then I took him back to his new home, where the same three people care for him, day in and day out. Where he is safe and feels secure. Where he is content. Where I visit him often.

Where, once a month, I pay rent.

"**rent** . . . *n* . . . **2 a** : . . . an agreed sum paid at fixed intervals by a tenant to the landlord"

Life Apart

And so it was that, after 30 years, we no longer shared a home. Did I miss Don? Wrenchingly.

Did I miss mopping up lakes of pee and failing at my attempts to create a quality of life for him? Not for a second.

I was like a raw wound, relieved to be able to begin my own healing and flinching at the pain I could only now start to examine. To look across the dining room table and not see him was like a small death. But he was not dead; only removed.

Acknowledging how much remained, I called it "widowhood with visiting privileges." Don was gone. He was not coming back. But I could still see him and get a hug. This, for me, was a gentler departure than if he had died suddenly. Dementia is cruel, but not without its blessings.

When I told people I had moved Don into foster care, kind friends, wanting to let me know they understood, related stories of relatives who had had to be placed in care. I listened, but to tell the truth, it was exhausting. I could not keep track of all those people I had never met. All I really wanted was for someone to ask how I was doing, so I could begin to make sense of my own reality.

Months before, a friend had described to me what it felt like, after years of heroic home care, to have placed her husband in a facility. She said, "I am free to be just a wife again." That proved to be my experience, as well. I took a perverse satisfaction in learning that, at the beginning, it was taking three people to give Don a shower. If he made a mess, it was no longer mine to clean up. I balanced my grief with newfound freedom.

I was lucky in that I did not mind living alone. I was 38 when I met Don. For much of my early adult life, I was on my own, so it was familiar territory. Thankfully, though, I'd learned some coping skills in the intervening years.

One thing I remembered was that, if I spent too much time alone, I tended to withdraw. So I made it a goal to have some sort of outside contact every day. To that end, I discovered the joys of exercise classes. They not only got me out amongst people, they also absolved me of needing to motivate myself to use the equipment in the basement. No longer did I have to expend vast amounts of energy on self pep talks. The social interactions with members of the class were a draw in themselves, every bit as important as the exercise.

While I already had several circles of friends—

church, music, book group, neighbors—I consciously added to them. This put structure into my life, as well as a cheerful abundance of connections.

And there were the frequent visits to see Don. At first, I went daily; later, I aimed for every other day. His care home was a mere 15 minutes away and not much impacted by rush hour traffic. This was fortunate, because often I would go before dinner, so the lure of food would distract him as I left. My presence was no competition for the dessert on his tray.

I read him children's stories, or we watched PBS Kids TV, or we looked at family photos or art books. I rarely took him on drives, because it was unpredictable whether he would cooperate about getting out of the car. He liked his new home, but he was still imprinted on me.

That being said, he loved colors. So as the seasons changed, we would take slow drives, to wonder at Nature's beauty or exclaim on displays of Christmas lights.

Occasionally, friends or family would come to see Don. I found that it was easiest for all concerned if I made a point to be there as well. By that time, Don was not very verbal, and my presence relieved the strain of conversation. I also functioned as an interpreter for Don, easing any fears that might arise. And in the end, we found he took as much pleasure in hearing us talk as he formerly would have as a participant.

Besides the time I spent with Don, keeping the house running, and professional commitments, I gave in to pampering myself. This felt like unalloyed luxury. Lying on the couch reading a book bordered on the sinfully delicious. Writing put me in a state of bliss. I was like a kid in a candy shop, wanting to sample all the sweets before deciding what to purchase.

In short, I was allowing myself to heal from the stress of caregiving and grieving.

Our 18-year-old cat kept me company, and, as her health began to fail, she became my old lady, showing me her vulnerability and letting me know when she was done with the last of her nine lives. She died a little over four months after Don moved out. I never told him.

I looked at my life and realized that, for the first time as an adult, I was not chasing a paycheck or a career, nor did I have anyone to take care of. It was as close to freedom as I might ever experience. Between music and writing, there were plenty of creative options. I had offers of jobs, but I found I didn't want to do the old familiar. This was my chance to explore and discover. It made me almost giddy.

The year 2019 was one of the best ever, full of newness and growth. Three friends and I formed a musical foursome. After decades of orchestral playing, doing chamber music, in which we each had our own part, gave free rein to my self-expression. That January, I also added two totally new experiences: I began learning taekwondo and signed up for my first creative writing class.

Meanwhile, it gave me great peace of mind to

know Don was being well cared for. Though I didn't want to be away for longer than a week at a time, there was a reassuring simplicity to being able to close up the house and venture off to see family or to perform out of town. I knew this year was a gift, and I was filled with gratitude for the rich possibilities.

Twice during 2019, I was able to bring Don home for gatherings of out-of-town family. It might seem strange that I did not do this more often, but I couldn't risk his reattaching himself to his former home. In fact, I don't know if he even recognized it as his own any more. The family and I carefully coordinated our arrivals and departures, so I wouldn't have to coax him back into the car alone. But to see him laughing and enjoying his young granddaughter was more precious than I can say.

They tell you caregivers should have their own support teams, something often overlooked in the minute-by-minute demands of tending to a person with dementia. While I gratefully accepted whatever help was offered, my team did not really take shape until after Don was in foster care. Family had been a big support, but they were not geographically close. Friends became more important than ever, and they proved champions.

But I would be remiss in not mentioning another companion. Early in Don's and my relationship, I had gotten a bear for my birthday. I've never been particularly captivated by stuffed animals, but Bear Stern immediately hopped up on the bed and began talking to us. Sometimes he would use my voice, sometimes Don's, but he had a knack for getting us to laugh, and he was also a very wise bear. So, in the spirit of full disclosure, I will tell you that crawling into bed at night and discussing the day with Bear gives me great comfort.

When you live alone, you can do these things, and no one is there to think you crazy.

Don , Holly, and Bear

In the End

What can I tell you about the end? That it went unbelievably fast? That, against expectations, it still came as a shock? That, to every appearance, he had the perfect death? All of these are true.

Aside from the dementia and recent, rather persistent, Urinary Tract Infections (UTI's), Don was, physically at least, quite healthy. He could still walk unaided, his blood pressure and cholesterol levels were stellar, and his few medications were mostly to ease the anxiety brought on by the Alzheimer's. I sometimes wondered if his body would long outlast his mind, a prospect I knew he would not have wanted.

But in the end, he traveled the path from decent health to death in a matter of days.

It was the first week of February, 2020. On Sunday, when I visited him, the new live-in caregiver said that, while she was cleaning Don's room, he'd told her, "You're a nice person." This, from someone who was almost non-verbal and who hadn't strung those particular words together in ages!

On Monday evening, I got a call that Don was having trouble keeping food down.

Tuesday, I made a doctor's appointment for the next day. I also called a hospice service, to find out how they worked, but wrote in my journal that I didn't think he was ready for hospice yet. I brought him some homemade yogurt and a tasty nutritional drink. He seemed to be experiencing a bit of pain from the UTI.

By Wednesday, he was too weak to go to his doctor's appointment. Still, I was totally blindsided when the owner of his care home said, "Come as soon as you can. I don't think he's going to last much longer." I called Don's daughter, so she and her husband could have one more visit. We contacted the hospice company, and they sent an intake nurse at one that afternoon.

In the midst of this, I was on the phone with Oregon Health & Science University (OHSU). Recently, I'd heard they were looking for body donations. Don had signed up decades earlier to be an organ donor, but at this stage, willing his brain and body to scientific research seemed more to the point. His daughter agreed that this was what he would have wanted.

It was a surreal day. I could tell Don was having to exert extra effort to cross the gap between us, to connect with me. His breathing sounded a bit congested, and he was a little clammy, but he no longer seemed to be in pain.

Oddly, though he was not aware of it, for the first time since the bird feeders had been placed outside his windows (a present from a close friend), the birds came to eat. After weeks of absence, the birds actually arrived! A corner of my brain made a note of it and was amazed.

When hospice and family had left and we were alone together, I got out my viola and played Bach's first cello suite for him, as I had when he first moved into foster care. I hoped it would soothe him. I could normally coax a smile out of him but had not, so far, been successful. He did seem calmer, though. And by the last two movements, the smile appeared. In retrospect, I think he was already beginning to transition. He was doing some unusual slow motion movements with his hands and arms, and the look on his face was one of wonder and happiness.

I did not spend the night with him, feeling I would be in the way of the caregivers, who planned to turn him every two hours. For some reason, I still thought death would take days or maybe weeks, or perhaps a different antibiotic would buy him more time. It seemed wiser to get a good night's sleep, so I could face decisions with an alert mind. Later in the evening, I got a hopeful text, with a photo, showing him sitting up and eating, looking more himself. I prayed he would wait for me.

But he did not. Just before 6:30 the next morning, I got the news that he had died during the night. I could do nothing but wail. It felt like a heavy door had slammed shut between us.

When I arrived at his care home, I was struck by

the expression on his face. He looked like he had just walked into a room and was delighted to see so many people he loved, greeting him. I could imagine his mother, her arms wide to welcome her son.

It was a crazy morning. I still needed to put things in place with OHSU, needed to let Don's family know he was gone, needed to tell my brother and a few key friends. My brother, bless him, overrode my hesitation and insisted he was flying up from Los Angeles immediately. He arrived a mere six hours later.

I took every opportunity I could, when there was a break in the phone calls and the questions, to crawl up beside Don and rest my head on his shoulder, to have one last chance to thank him and tell him how much I was going to miss him. Those were some of the most precious moments of my life.

And then, incredibly, by 11 a.m., the mortuary service for OHSU was there to take Don away. My generous husband still had one more gift to bestow.

Even though I felt part of me had been zipped into that body bag, I had to acknowledge Don had probably had the most perfect death he could have wished for. Aside from the Alzheimer's, he had no prolonged illness. He made his exit while he could still enjoy the people around him, before the disease got really ugly. And he appeared to have died peacefully in his sleep. Though I deeply regretted not being with him when he transitioned, I wonder if that would have made it harder for him, if he would have felt torn between moving ahead or staying with me.

When the COVID-19 virus shutdown hit about five weeks later, I was even more grateful Don died when he did. I cannot imagine the agony and confusion he would have experienced, not being able to see me, with no understanding of what was causing the absence. My heart ached for those who lost dear ones and could not, as I did, lie down beside them for one last visit. And months later, after two trips to see family had to be canceled due to the pandemic, I realized Don had given my brother and me one last present: the four days we had together immediately following his death.

Once again, amid choices I would not willingly have made, I found I had been blessed.

Uncharted Territory

Many people have clear beliefs about what happens after a person dies. This was not us. With my upbringing, and as Unitarian Universalists, Don and I enjoyed exploring the possibilities.

We often read books on the subject, ranging from Eben Alexander's *Proof of Heaven* to several by Rosemary Altea, a practicing medium, as well as many others. We took a trip to Brazil, to see the medium and psychic surgeon John of God and to ponder the existence of unseen Entities. This gave us an even wider view of how the Universe *might* operate. I found it surprisingly comforting to embrace the mystery.

Then there were the personal experiences. Don had felt, on two occasions, the presence of friends who had died, who came to reassure him that they were all right. We also had the account of Don's uncle, who had died on the operating table. The uncle described floating above his inert body, watching the doctors trying to revive him, while he was being pulled toward the tunnel of light. He felt completely at peace and would have gladly continued, except for the knowledge that his wife still needed him. And so he returned to inhabit his body. He said after that, he was never afraid.

Now I was facing the death of the person I knew perhaps better than I'd ever known anyone. Where had he gone? Was he whole and healthy again? Was part of him still with me, only now unseen? In the midst of my grief, I wondered.

Not long after he died, I had a dream. We were cruising down a sunny highway in a 1970s station wagon, with Don at the wheel and me behind him, in the back seat. All of a sudden, I realized this might not be a safe situation. "Are you supposed to be driving?" I asked. Don turned to look at me, unalloyed bliss on his face. "Oh, I'm fine now," he said. Was this just wishful thinking on my part or...?

Which is not to discredit wishful thinking. Much as swelling around a wound protects it, our minds find ways to guard against total devastation in the face of trauma. Again, I found the questions more comforting than an absolute truth, because of the infinite possibilities.

What I did find unsettling was the concept that Don might indeed still be nearby, as Canon Henry Scott Holland had written a century earlier (see "Full House?" following this chapter). The corollary to this idea was how upsetting it would be to Don if I did not acknowledge him. So I went looking.

I found him when I needed him most. In those first months of grief, and later, when I could use his help.

A river stone, shaped almost like a heart, became a message of love. It was blue, Don's favorite color. The shadows of aspen leaves dancing on the grass were his greeting. Those were trees I had planted nearly three decades earlier, volunteer saplings from his youth church camp in Idaho. The brilliance of sunshine on the river reminded me of the warming power of his love. A pair of birds on bare branches signified our years of companionship.

One night, I asked for Don's assistance when my wallet went missing. I am not prone to misplacing important things, and I was very clear on where and when I'd last had it. But to be safe, I went online and checked my credit card action. Nothing out of order so far. As I was closing out the computer, Don's picture came up, so I asked if he could help me find the wallet. Retracing my steps, it seemed logical that it must have dropped out of my hand in the closet, but I'd already checked the floor. Then I noticed the bag of birthday presents waiting to be delivered to a friend. It was covered with tissue paper. Could it be possible...? I lifted off the top layer, and there was my wallet!

Now I don't want to get too weird here, but really, what's the harm in believing the best? And gratitude, even to someone who is no longer visibly present, is never amiss.

I mentioned earlier that, when I first heard Don had died, it felt like a heavy door had slammed shut. Thinking back on the text message that bore the news, I remember seeing the word "passed" and feeling a nanosecond of relief. While it is not unusual for someone who has cared for an ill person to have a sense of liberation, I was no longer on the front line of caregiving. Nor was I tired of going to visit him. So I wanted to look more closely at this first reaction.

What I found was two-fold. The first was relief at knowing how it turned out. It felt like I had been holding my breath for years, wondering where this disease was going to take us. The second was relief that neither Don nor I had to go the route of prolonged disintegration. In a sense, we had been spared.

Then the door closed, and I mourned the fact that I would no longer be able to make new memories with this man I so loved. Although, whether by actuality or deluded imagination, this has not proved to be true for me. He is still very much a part of my life.

There is perhaps no time when you are more fragile than when you have just faced a great loss. Aside from the deaths of my elderly parents and two geriatric cats, I had only looked at grief from the outside, never knowing quite what to say when others were bereaved. Don's death was unlike anything I'd ever experienced.

What did I learn from it?

Let me first say I truly felt the love and support of people who were trying to comfort me. And yet, I stumbled over their words. I was so edgy I wanted to edit much of what was said. I was well aware it was a blessing that Don did not outlive his capacity to take joy in life. And when the pandemic and the shutdown set in, I was grateful he had escaped a situation that would have been extremely traumatic for both of us. But when others voiced those very same thoughts, it rankled. It seemed as if they were saying—though I knew they were not—that there was less need for me to feel bad. I was the one who had been through the storm, and I wanted to claim my own silver lining. I plead temporary insanity for my reactions. They were no one's fault but my own.

More than anything—more than well-chosen expressions of solace—I needed people to ask, "How are you doing?" and then just listen while I worked through this strange terrain. For me, as a person who devours life through language, words were my lifeline. But they needed to be mine.

As for important dates on the calendar—Valentine's Day, wedding anniversary, birthdays, holidays—they all happen, even after someone dies. It's not like you're apt to unearth new pain by asking, "How are you?" It may elicit some tears, but that's okay. At least, that's how I felt.

I do recognize we all have varying reactions to grief, and someone else might feel entirely different. I can only speak for myself. In the end, whatever was said or left unsaid, I was immeasurably grateful for the love and friendship people offered me. And who knows? My experience may make me even more tongue-tied in the face of others' grief than I was before. At the very least, it has definitely heightened my curiosity about how people handle their own losses.

Interestingly, I had no inclination whatsoever to read about the process of grieving. I found I had no interest in reducing it to five stages I could then check off, as if on a to-do list. I did not want to "understand" it in a clinical sense. I needed instead to venture, unguided, into this new terrain.

And what I have found there has been surprisingly rich and beautiful.

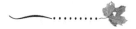

FULL HOUSE?

Look, here's the deal. I try to keep an open mind about things. I was raised by a cultural anthropologist father and a free-thinking educator mother, grew up exposed to people from many countries and beliefs, and ended up a Unitarian Universalist. For me, there is no one way to look at life.

Or death.

My husband died a few weeks ago. When I heard the news, it felt like a heavy door had slammed shut. It took me several days to figure out that what bothered me most was that it had shut out the possibility of making new memories with this man I had so loved for over 32 years.

Then a friend sent me a beautiful quote from Canon Henry Scott Holland, something written over a century ago:

> *"Death is nothing at all. I have slipped away into the next room. I am I, and you are you. Whatever we were to each other, that we are still. Call me by my old familiar name, speak to me in the easy way which you always used. Put no difference in your tone, wear no forced air of solemnity or sorrow. Laugh as we always laughed, at the little jokes we enjoyed together. Pray, smile, think of me, pray for me. Let my name be the household word that it always was. Let it be spoken without effect, without trace of shadow on it. Life means all that it ever meant, it is*

the same as it ever was, there is an unbroken continuity.
What is death but a negligible accident? Why should I be
out of mind because I am out of sight? I am waiting for
you for an interval, somewhere very near, just around the
corner.
  "All is well."

It got me to wondering if my husband really were still with
me, trying to get my attention, trying to let me know he was
finally well and whole again, that he was proud of me.
I asked him for a sign, and on a hike with a friend, along a
riverbank strewn with stones of many colors, I picked up a
blue one–his favorite color–and found it was in the shape of
a heart.

Now, it's not your perfectly symmetrical heart. It's more
artistic than that. And some might say I'm reading into the
slight slope at the top a shape that isn't there. But I am not
easily dissuaded from this sign of love.

What if he is still here and I just can't see him? The thought
of him trying to communicate and me not listening is heart
wrenching. Besides, I don't want to miss any of his jokes…
or his smile…or his laughter.

And if he is still here, how long will he stay? Are there others
with him? Our parents, perhaps? Our two kitties? Just how
crowded is this "next room"?

Is it possible I am living in a full house, without my even
knowing it?

(DIS)APPEARING ACTS?

It is nearly six months since your final Disappearing Act, though in truth you had been slowly vanishing for many years, smudging around the edges of your vibrant personality, till one day we sat, with no words, and simply stared into each other's eyes, nodding slightly from time to time, to acknowledge the arc of our love. Not long after, you left for good.

Or did you?

One morning recently, I sat outside eating breakfast, feasting on the view of the garden. As the sun came up behind me and crested the hedge, something yellow caught my eye (a butterfly? a leaf?). It disappeared before I could identify it, but in its place was the magic of the lawn, alive with the shadows of dancing aspen leaves, as if you had your hands held high, waving at me, saying, "I am here! Keep looking and you will know my presence."

A couple of weeks later, on an early morning bike ride, an unoccupied dock beckoned me to sit by the river. And so I did, blessed by the water and the birds and the quiet. As I stood to leave, the river was ebullient with shards of light. It felt as if you had thrown the electricity of your love upon the water, to let me know that part of you was still very much alive.

So here we are, with this mystery between us. Are you gone, or are these your Appearing Acts?

IRONY

You died eleven days ago.

This morning your frequent flyer account
Emailed to offer you 40,000 more miles.
It gave me a much needed laugh.

Where would you go with those 40,000 miles
When planes are no longer of use to you?
When I want so badly to have you here by my side
Healthy and whole again
So that we could laugh together
At the ironies of life.

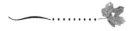

SITTING

I sit
On this Sunday before Thanksgiving
This Sunday before your birthday
My heart bruised from a dream in which
I could not find you

I sit
With the morning's church service
Live-streaming
And think of your death

I sit
As the pianist plays the Air from Bach's Third Suite
A favorite of yours
And see a lone bird
Perched at the top of
A tall tree
Bare branches etching the sky
And I miss you
With an ache so deep
I am rooted in grief

I sit
Until I notice
A second bird
Waiting

A few branches down
Until
At the last notes of the Air
They fly off together

I sit
And see
One lone leaf
Waving at me

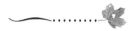

GREETING

On this first anniversary of your death
I awoke to a slivered moon
Winking out from its winter quilt
A jaunty bedcap of light
I took as a greeting

If I closed one eye, you were over there
If I closed the other, I was here
With both eyes open
We strode the heavens in tandem
Two waning crescents
Apart
Until I focused us into one

Is this how death works?
Not lack of existence
But the inability to be seen?

I have filled this dreaded day
With people who knew you well
In hopes that cushions of laughter
Will soften my sorrow
And let you wax again
Into the fullness of being

Grieving During a Pandemic

T here was plenty of grief to go around in the year 2020. COVID-19 was turning everyone's life upside down, mine included. Don's death just added another layer of heartache. His demise, though not unexpected, was nonetheless devastating. Looking back, I find it hard to distinguish which emotions pertained to my bereavement and which to the global catastrophe.

Here in the United States, the mid-March shutdown hit about five weeks after Don died. By that time, I had taken care of most of the required paperwork and was trying to keep my life moving forward as best I could. Now I was facing a dozen days of disparate music rehearsals and performances.

Being a professional violinist and singing in my church choir is an enjoyable combination of music making...until they try to occupy the same time frame. The upcoming schedule required traveling, both solo and orchestral violin playing, and choral singing. To add further challenge, one of the choir pieces was about someone who had recently died. I've never figured out how to cry and sing at the same time.

There was a question, lurking somewhere in the back of my mind, whether packing so much into such a short period was a good idea...especially with the diversity of the commitments and out-of-town travel ...especially with my raw grief. Performing usually feels to me a bit like a high wire act, and Don's death inserted a whole new magnitude of possibilities to fall, to fail.

But beginning on the evening of March 11th, and over the next couple of days, everything was canceled. By March 16th, we were totally shut down.

Don's Celebration of Life, which I'd set for the end of April, got moved to September 20th, the 33rd anniversary of our meeting. Then that, too, went by the wayside. I was offered a Zoom memorial service, but I remained adamant about waiting until we could gather in person to give him a good send-off. People talk about "closure," but I was in no hurry to close this chapter of my life.

What the pandemic did give me was time. And quiet. Space to process my loss. Over the past decade, I'd promised myself that, after Don died, I would write a book about our Alzheimer's experience. I dove in, putting on paper the thoughts and stories that had been rambling through my brain. The writing gave a fullness to our history and excavated memories of my healthy husband before the disease. By sharing, I hoped I could help someone else dealing with a loved one's dementia.

I needed to cope with the fact that life without people to bump up against was truly weird. They say you learn by going off course and then correcting. But what if there are no guardrails when you veer too far in one direction? People were my guardrails. And I still had to find a way to navigate this thing called grief.

Fortunately, my friends were game for walking or bike riding. We masked up, physically distanced, and went out, rain or shine. Sometimes we would get Thai food and eat it in my backyard. That area became my living room, until it was too cold and damp to be really enjoyable. Happily, other friends had covered patios, sometimes even heated and furnished with electric blankets.

For a brief while, during good weather, I gave "open window" concerts on my violin. I texted my neighbors that, at 5:15 p.m., I would open my windows and give a short performance. It was my way of offering an uplifting counterbalance to the pandemic that was slowly eroding our lives. Friends (and sometimes passersby) would gather in my driveway, a few with a festive glass of wine in hand, to let the music work its wonders.

Unfortunately, it was too soon after Don's death for me to sustain the amount of energy performing requires. Grief regained the upper hand. At one point, it felt like I had crashed into a wall. A blank wall. I decided not to fight it. It may have been gardening season, but I had hit a fallow period.

As the pandemic shutdown continued, I freaked out

when I realized suddenly that I had not touched another living being in over two months! Grieving is one thing; isolation is another. They do not make good companions.

It was obviously time to replace our cat, Misty, who had died nearly two years earlier. I was not alone in my search for a pet, however. Adoption proved trickier than normal, as the animal shelters were flooded with requests. It seemed I would never make it to the top of the adoption list.

A friend had recommended I get an adult male cat, as they are often extremely affectionate, but none of the males offered at the time sounded like the right fit. Most were either too old or with medical problems (I was not in a rescuing frame of mind at that point). In desperation, I asked Don if he could help find me a good kitty. You never know what powers the deceased might possess, and I was open to all the help I could get. Sitting down again at my computer, I decided there were two "somewhat" possibilities, so I filled out questionnaires for both.

The following day, I got a call from the Humane Society. I had made it to the top of the list! The cat in question did not have a good PR photo. Someone had given him a lion cut, with fur on only his head, legs, and the end of his tail. He was a mystery kitty; little was known about his past. BUT, he was in good health, about a year old, and very affectionate. I signed up for a meet-and-greet the next day. As I drove him home from the shelter, I introduced him to Beethoven's Second Symphony on the radio and was pleased to discover my new housemate did not object to classical music. This was an excellent sign.

For those of you with inquiring minds, Theo the Cat's fur grew out, not all at once, but beginning at the nape of his neck and slowly inching its way toward his tail. Meanwhile, on the tail, the fur crept down from the end "poof," till the two camps met about an inch south of his body. In a shutdown, you have time to notice these things, and I'm happy to report that isolation is so much more manageable when you have a cat purring against you.

Then there were the Zoom meetings. God bless ingenuity! Suddenly the world was coming into our homes. This suited the part of me that hates wasted effort. Now I could take classes, listen to concerts, and join groups without having to commute. Learning about racial injustice and spiritual deepening was a fine use of a year when most of my music-making (aside from a virtual choir) was put on hold. In a way, I was growing myself out of my grief. And I could feel Don cheering me on.

Which makes me wonder, *How might I have fared without the shutdown?* That time was immeasurably rich for me. I now have many new friends, a more profound appreciation of the importance of connectedness, and a realization of what I need for a good mental outlook. Had life proceeded at its normal pace, I might have spent much more effort in just trying to keep up, nibbling away at my grief in between other activities.

I don't want in any way to minimize the heartbreak

and devastation COVID-19 has wreaked on the world. This is not an attempt to glory in the shutdown. I was simply fortunate that the time and space it afforded me was exactly what I needed to deal with my own private grief.

Lessons Learned

Gratitude

I learned my most valuable lesson when I started going to an Alzheimer's support group in March of 2016. Don was still living at home, and I was having trouble navigating his altered behavior. I noticed that most of the people in the meeting were caring for someone who was much farther along the path than Don was at that time. The message to me was clear: what I had then was as good as it was going to get. I needed to cherish what I still had. I did not want to spend the rest of our time together looking over my shoulder, regretting what we'd lost and missing whatever joy we could still share.

I was not naturally a glass-half-full person. I think being an artist of any sort makes you focus on how things can be improved. It's a bit of an occupational hazard. But dealing with my husband's mental and physical decline was a huge wake-up call. I could either bemoan what wasn't working or celebrate any small triumph I could wrest from this downward spiral.

And so I began to sift through the rubble of our lives, mining for glints of gold.

I had not realized how much I had incorporated this new outlook, until the day I was visiting with a close friend of ours. She began to talk about how she was mourning the loss of the Don we both knew. *Don't go there!!!* my brain screamed. I said nothing, realizing she needed to give voice to her feelings, but it highlighted for me that my new perspective was essential for my own mental health.

With Alzheimer's, as with most things, there will be good days and not-so-good days. The trick, I found, was to celebrate the good ones, to realize that they were better and therefore something to be grateful for. When you are caring for someone with dementia, it's like being dealt a hand of cards you would rather put back in the deck. And yet, along the way I saw that, given my hand, there was always one card that offered the best play.

Perhaps I was just lucky. I have listened to people's stories and sat in awe of their struggles. I've watched them face their problems with heroic strength. It's not an easy road, but it breaks us open to reservoirs of endurance, compassion, and gratitude we might never have known.

What was I most grateful for? It changed with the stages of decline. When Don was still living at home, a good night's sleep was a miracle. My husband, it seemed, had perfected the torture of sleep deprivation. Sometime during the night, he would whisper something, which would wake me up. "What did you say?" I'd ask. But either he could not remember or had dozed off. At which point, I would spend the next two or three hours trying to get back to sleep, only to be awakened by another whisper.

I rejoiced when his brain worked well enough that there was still the possibility of meaningful conversation, however brief. When I could take him to a respite group and have him tell me afterward that he'd had a good time, even if he couldn't remember what they'd done. When we'd get in the car and he'd look over, a smile on his face, and say, "I have the best chauffeur in the world!"

Some of my favorite times together in the last years of Don's life were when we went on drives to see the spring blossoms or fall leaves. "Oh, look!" I'd say. And Don would respond breathlessly, wonder in his voice, "Yeah!" Or, if the explosion of color were really spectacular, he would laugh and clap his hands. I have never experienced Nature with such an open heart as I did on those slow drives down back roads, seeing the world through my husband's eyes. It was one of the blessings we wrested from the grip of Alzheimer's.

Shared laughter was something I missed terribly as Don declined. From the day we met, we realized how well matched our senses of humor were. We loved puns, the ironies of life, quirky ways of looking at the world. But as the developmental clock rolled back, he became—like a child—more literal, and the subtleties eluded him.

So I cherish the last time Don realized I was

teasing him. I was sitting beside him, feeding him his dinner, and since he subscribed to the adage "Eat dessert first!" we were working on a piece of cake. As I filled the second spoonful, I said, "Oh, that smells wonderful! Maybe I should help you eat it." I was looking at his profile and saw everything stop. No chewing, no motion. Then slowly, the corner of his eye crinkled up, and he turned to look at me, silent laughter on his face. We had triumphed once more.

Although I would never wish Alzheimer's on anyone, without the disease that final bit of humor would have been so commonplace I probably wouldn't have noticed it. Now it was a supreme gift.

Besides laughter, we also shared music. It always amazed me that, two days before we met, he had attended his first performance of an orchestra I played in. Over the years I used to joke that we couldn't start a concert until "Mom" was in his seat. He was my biggest fan.

With age, higher pitches became hard on him. Still, he continued to sit close to me when I practiced at home, his hands over his ears. I would suggest he'd be more comfortable across the room, but he rarely moved. Thus, the first time I played for him after he moved into foster care, I brought my viola (which is lower pitched than the violin) and put on my heavy mute to dampen the sound. I was part way through Bach's first cello suite (transcribed for viola) when he got out of his chair, walked over to his bed, and pulled up the covers. I worried that he was trying to escape the sound, so at the end of the first movement, I went over to ask if he was okay. "Yes," he said, scrunching up his eyes. "I love you!"

AUTUMN GRACE

Yesterday the leaves fell with ebullient fantasy
A ballerina in full pirouette
A toboggan bounding over leaf drifts
A pilot practicing touch-and-goes

We watched through the windshield
The car stopped, not parked,
On a quiet neighborhood street
And laughed in appreciation
(As one might at fireworks)
To see autumn's unexpected display

And this I knew was a gift
A holy moment we could share
Even, and because of,
Your own fantastical path
With Alzheimer's

THANKSGIVING

On Thanksgiving Day, my husband will have been in foster care for 18 months. A year-and-a-half.

I miss his laughter. I miss doing things with him–going for walks, bike rides, hikes. Sharing meals and chores. I miss seeing him in the audience when I perform.

And yet.

And yet, I can still visit him. He is close by. I can walk into his room and watch his smile light up the world. On good days, he might even manage a hug, and if I am lucky, a strong one, confirming we are connected.

I can't remember the last time he said my name. He is not very verbal, where once he was loquacious. He used to write poetry. We even wrote a mystery novel together, though not to perfection. We both loved words and puns and humor. And now, for the most part, he is silent.

And yet.

And yet, he knows I am someone special in his life. I tell him I am his wife. Explain we have been in love for 32 years. Not long ago, after I'd said this, a radiant look of recognition beamed, as he proclaimed, triumphantly, "You're mine!"

I am on a slow walk to widowhood, each decline a reminder that this journey does not have a happy ending.

And yet.

And yet, the inevitable is doled out in small doses, allowing me time to digest the fragments. He is content and well cared for, and I am free to be just a wife. Life is full again. And I have discovered a depth of compassion, caring, and love from our friends that I might not otherwise have known. These are blessings hard won.

Yes, he may not speak much. And yet, he remembers how to say, "I love you."

In between what is and what might never have been, lies gratitude.

Safety and Health

I had never participated in a support group until Don got dementia. Now I wonder how I would have survived without them. They helped me navigate the challenges with all sorts of practical advice.

I joined two, each meeting once a month. It was interesting to notice their differences, as well as their similarities. In one of them, the members had a strong desire to exchange recommendations of books they'd read on the subject; in the other, we traded experiences and suggestions. But both of them allowed us the opportunity to talk about our struggles and to gain the wisdom of those farther down the path. Even after our loved one died, many of us continued to go, to stay in touch and to help those still dealing with this awful disease.

Keeping a person with dementia safe is tricky, because behavior is so unpredictable. You might think one day that your husband would never do thus-and-so, only to be proven wrong the next. And adults, with their greater stature and skills, can get into much more trouble than a toddler.

One hurdle is removing the car keys. While Don was at the stage of Mild Cognitive Impairment, a medical social worker explained to me that, if we were in a car accident and Don was driving, the financial consequences could be devastating. Don had had some worrisome outings when he got lost en route to once-familiar places, but he was still a good driver as long as I was there to navigate, and he loved driving. I was grateful that the monetary explanation for why he needed to give it up made sense to him. He acquiesced gracefully. Don did not want to be a financial burden to me.

That was our story. We were lucky. Others had to have a doctor write to the Department of Motor Vehicles, to require that the person take a driving test. Or they would disable the car by removing a crucial part, though this was not practical if the healthy person needed to use that car. Hiding the car keys had spotty success. My only recommendation is to try to get the soon-to-be-ex-driver on your side. Make that person a participant in the decision, if at all possible.

I was also fortunate in that Don was not a wanderer. The only times he roamed, he was looking for me.

The first occasion was perfectly logical, but absolutely terrifying. We were in St. Louis, Missouri, for a conference. We had been there many times, but the city now had new restaurants to explore.

After dinner near the Convention Center before an evening meeting, Don went to use the bathroom.

What I did not know was that the facilities were in a central area, serving several businesses. Don had not left bread crumbs to guide him back. Finding the men's room was easy; knowing which way to go when he was done was unfathomable.

Out into the rainy night he went, in search of me. Nothing looked familiar. I, meanwhile, was wondering what was taking so long, so I went to investigate. The security guard for the building checked the empty restroom and other businesses and accompanied me to the Convention Center. I tried calling Don's cell numerous times but was getting no answer. At this stage, using the phone was difficult for Don, so I'd programmed his for one-button dialing to reach me. I kept trying.

Finally, after the eternity of a half-hour of searching, his name lit up my screen! He was six long blocks away, at the downtown grocery store, soaking wet. Could I please come get him. My new best friend, the security guard, insisted on walking me over, telling me en route about his grandfather, who'd had Alzheimer's and one night walked 20 miles into the city center. It was comforting to be with someone who understood what I was going through.

When I got Don back to the hotel and tucked into bed, I told him I needed to go downstairs for a few minutes. Though I'd stayed unemotional up to that point, I now felt I was about to jump out of my skin. I desperately needed someone to talk to and could only do that out of earshot of Don. I went to the lobby and started calling family and friends. With each unsuccessful try, my tamped-down hysteria ratcheted up.

At last I connected with a friend who knew us well. "We're okay," I said, before I dissolved into uncontrollable sobs. She waited me out, and when I was finally able to talk, she listened. Eventually, I calmed down, but the horror of that experience stayed with me.

One other instance Don "wandered" was when I was at choir practice. As I turned onto our street, coming home, I saw a familiar figure in the dark, walking in the road, one of our business cards held out in front of him like a talisman.

"Where are you going?" I asked.

"To find you," he responded.

After that, I became religious about leaving him a note, saying where I was and when I'd be back. That seemed to work for him. Over time, I amassed a stack of such notes, which I would simply recycle as the situation required.

Knowing where I was, however, didn't prevent every disaster.

It was July 15, 2017, and we had just gotten back from a trip to Los Angeles. I had a short turnaround time, before I needed to play at a wedding. I got Don situated, and a friend picked me up, so we could carpool downtown.

When we returned three hours later, Don met me with a worried look. "I have something to show you," he said, and led me down the hall. Liquid was coming out of the downstairs bedroom. When I opened the door, a torrent of water tumbled from the ceiling and continued into the basement.

I rushed upstairs and discovered Don had managed to plug up the toilet and then flushed it in such a way that the water continued to run. My once handy husband no longer knew to jiggle the handle or shut off the valve. Alzheimer's had stolen that part of his brain.

Fortunately, our insurance company took good care of us. As I called to open the claim, I told them, "I have a husband with dementia and an elderly cat. I'm going to need some help with this." And, bless them, they gave us much-appreciated consideration. For the next 4 1/2 months, they housed us, first in a nice residential hotel and then in a beautiful brand-new apartment overlooking the Willamette River, accommodations that provided a great deal of solace for us both.

Before signing the lease, I brought Don to look at the apartment, so he'd have a sense of where we were going from the hotel. On the way back, I asked what he thought. "Can't we stay where we are?" he responded. When I inquired what he was going to miss about the hotel, he made an obscure gesture in front of him and slightly over his head.

Now, by this time, I was getting pretty good at interpreting his sign language. Though we were in the car, I knew he was indicating the top of the refrigerator in our mini kitchen. And on top of the refrigerator was where the remainder of a luscious chocolate cake was residing! "Don't worry," I said. "We'll take the cake with us."

We were now okay to move.

It was while we were in that apartment that I realized Don had not entirely given up cooking. I awoke one morning to discover a package of veggie burgers on the stove, next to a frying pan. Apparently, my husband had gotten hungry in the night and made himself a burger. True, he didn't remember to put the remaining burgers back in the freezer, but at least he hadn't burned the place down.

I have this view of life I call the Inoculation Theory: when the Universe sends you a warning, it's important to take heed. In this case, I learned to remove the knobs from the stove unless I was cooking. We didn't need a fire on top of the flood.

Keeping your loved one (and perhaps you) safe at home requires that you think with the mind of a very young person in the body of a grown-up. I have known people who had to hide the kitchen knives as the disease progressed. Fortunately, the only time I felt physically threatened was the occasional push when I was trying to shower Don, and I made sure to position myself so a shove would do little damage. But you can never totally let down your guard, and you are well advised to think ahead for potential dangers. These are some of the more exhausting aspects of caregiving for a person with dementia.

This same vigilance is required when you are

out in public. I sometimes had to intervene when a stranger did not understand why Don did not respond normally to casual banter. Or when Don felt obliged to tell someone how bad smoking was for them as we passed them in the street. He became the tattoo police and the arbiter of weight control, with no attempt to keep his comments at a whisper. In our trigger-happy society, people have been shot for erratic behavior caused by mental illness. And dementia is indeed a mental illness.

Unfortunately, as dementia progresses it also affects the physical. It makes it harder for your loved one to tell you they hurt and where the pain is. There were numerous times when Don's behavior became unusually bizarre or when I thought he was on a precipitous downhill slide, only to discover he had a Urinary Tract Infection. I soon learned to have this checked first, before looking for other causes. When the doctors were able to match the bacteria with the proper antibiotic, within days I would get my husband back. I also learned to request that they culture his urine, because sometimes the initial analysis does not detect the bacteria.

I found taking Don to a doctor's appointment to be a monumental challenge. The people at the foster home could help me get him into the car, but when we arrived at the medical office, getting Don out of the car was well nigh impossible. One time, the doctor made a "car call," when there was no way to budge him. Sometimes I could cajole him inside, but then something seemingly simple, like stepping onto a scale, might be insurmountable.

The medical staff were usually accommodating. One particularly kind example was with our dentist. Don was having silver fluoride applied to some cavities. This is a new option to avoid the drilling process, which would have been terrifying to my husband. But this method requires several visits to build it up.

We were there for the final application. Don could not be persuaded to get out of the car. I asked the dental assistant if she could work her charm on him —by this time, we knew all these people quite well— but her efforts also came to naught. So, in the end, we got curbside service. The dental assistant moved into the driver's seat, with me in the back seat behind her, to keep Don calm. We reclined Don's seat, and the dentist leaned in, with another assistant outside the car, bearing the fluoride and any equipment needed. Sometimes it does indeed take a village.

Curbside service

The Best, and Sometimes the Only, Medicine

Dementia and stress bring out rich possibilities for laughter. Support group sessions often dissolved into giggles over someone's recounting of the latest mishaps. One frequent topic: "Pee and Poop." You would not believe the number of receptacles (and other locations) that a diseased mind views as an appropriate place to urinate. If you find your heating vents, corners of the carpet, or buckets beginning to reek, I recommend you investigate. I once went for days checking the plumbing, wondering why our bathroom smelled more and more like sewage...until I remembered a middle-of-the-night sound of liquid cascading into a plastic wastebasket.

Don's altered perception of the world around him and the fact that his filters of social appropriateness had vanished made for many truly funny situations. The incongruities always caught me by surprise, and what was there to do but laugh?

The last year he lived at home, I usually brought Don along to choir rehearsals. He loved the music, even though when we sopranos went into the stratosphere, he had to cover his ears against the high pitches. He sat out in the sanctuary and would often join in from afar on our warm-up exercises, a look of earnest concentration on his face, singing just slightly behind the rest of us. Happily, the choir director and my fellow choristers loved him too much to mind, and we still chuckle over his participation.

One evening we were rehearsing a piece that called for choir, piano, and solo saxophone. Our choir director had decided to put the sax player in the balcony, above and behind Don. The piano was playing, the choir was singing, and then the instrumental solo began. Immediately, Don whipped around in his seat and yelled, "SHUT UP!!!" My hero, my protector! The memory makes me laugh even now. Fortunately, as so often happens, I discovered the young sax player had a grandmother with dementia. He was unfazed and hadn't missed a note.

Another source of humor was the irresistible allure of desserts. For some reason, dementia seems to bring out the sweet tooth in people. Unfortunately, refined sugar also causes inflammation, including in the brain, which is detrimental for keeping the synapses working. So I frequently told Don he needed to avoid having too many sweets.

They say people do not remember what you say, but they do remember how you made them feel. Sugar made Don feel happy. Though he might not be able to find any number of things in the house, he always knew where the candy was stored. (I know, I should have just hidden the treats, but I was still hoping for enlightenment on his part. That's how brain-addled caregivers can become!)

One day, I'd been given a bag of gourmet desserts, among which were a shortbread cookie with sugary icing and a bar of special chocolate. I don't like sweet things, but I love good chocolate. Don and I had sampled both, and I was looking forward to savoring the rest of the bar over the next week.

Then I went outside to shovel a rare snowfall off our sidewalks. Since our house is on a corner lot, there was a lot of pavement to clear. I came in quite a bit later, sweaty and tired. Don met me with the proud announcement that he hadn't eaten the cookie, because it had too much sugar in it. "But," he said, "the chocolate didn't have any." When I retrieved the empty wrapper from recycling, I pointed out that sugar was at the top of the list of ingredients hidden beneath the fold in the paper. Alas, it was too late.

The combination of incongruity and surprise again caught me off guard when a fellow musician and dear friend provided a rare social outing for Don. We were invited to lunch at her house, after which we would serenade him with violin duets.

Don had a special technique when it came to desserts in those last years. He would eat his as fast as he could, and then look meaningfully at mine. At least I wasn't going to get fat, married to him.

After I'd finished what was left of my dessert, our friend and I played a Mozart duo, with her dog, Sandy, stretched out at Don's feet. Both seemed happy to listen to us. Which made Don's comment afterward all the funnier. "I don't see how Sandy puts up with it," he said, as my friend and I laughed till the tears ran. To this day, that phrase still gets us going.

Not many months before Don died, I brought him home for a family gathering. We were celebrating five birthdays, so of course there was birthday cake. I sat next to Don, to feed him. No sooner was his piece gone, than he shifted his gaze longingly at my plate. I shared. Then he spotted our five-year-old granddaughter's piece at the far end of the dining room table. She had eaten off the "wedding cream" (her term for whipped cream) and was poking at the cake which had supported it, obviously not making much progress. I looked at Don beside me. His profile reminded me of the lizards you see on nature programs, unmoving and fully focused on their prey. Thankfully, Don's tongue did not stretch that far.

The unpredictability of dementia will catch you off guard in a nanosecond. It will have you looking at life in ways you might never otherwise have thought of. Suddenly the world shifts, and before you've had time to regain your balance, you find yourself laughing uproariously. Those moments belong in your display case of small triumphs.

Do-Overs and Take-Aways

I am not usually a person who looks over her shoulder, second-guessing decisions. I figure we do the best we can with the information we have at the time, and hindsight, while it might be enlightening, should not be used against us.

That being said, if I were to do it over again—which, thankyouverymuch, once really was enough—I would work harder at trying to see things through Don's eyes. But when you are up to your tush in alligators, these finer points fall by the wayside. It was much easier to contemplate them when someone else was doing the caregiving.

As I mentioned earlier, reconciling an adult body with the mind of a child was a lesson I was slow to learn. All my years of teaching students to play the violin told me that if I just found the right way to explain to my husband what he should do, he could still _____ (fill in the blank). Hah! The new me would give him a much simpler task and praise him profusely for completing even a part of it. This would have made us both happy.

Looking back at those times, I see my husband trying desperately to succeed in a world that was no longer comprehensible. This took the somewhat amusing form of herding our cat. No sooner did Misty come in from the outdoors than Don would turn into her personal traffic bobby. "No, Misty, don't go there!"...as she sashayed across the living room to her couch. It's a wonder she didn't need a pet psychologist, with all that helpful direction, but I think it gave Don a sense of being in control of something, even if he wasn't successful.

It would have been useful had I recognized sooner the underlying fear that prompted his bizarre behavior. I guess I assumed this was the new Don, and I would have to learn to live with it, though I fervently hoped it was just a phase. Had I not been so overwhelmed, I might have taken more time to address his fears, to reassure him he was safe, to explain the unexplainable. To distract him. To simply cuddle him.

Anti-anxiety medications gave Don the chance to live more comfortably in a world that was increasingly hard for him to understand. His caregivers, bless them, made sure he wasn't overmedicated. I never saw him sedated, as I have heard can happen in larger facilities if the staff-to-patient ratio is inadequate.

As time passed, the slow drives we took down the back roads, to look at spring and autumn colors, got increasingly uncomfortable for Don. He somehow felt the need to help me drive, to keep us safe. He would gesture to a stop sign half a block away, rather than enjoying the sights. For those occasions, I wish I had given him a bit of CBD oil, to relax him. We were hardly in any danger, at 15 mph.

This is the question: at what point do enriching experiences become a source of discomfort? "Enriching" suggests something out of the ordinary, which can easily be scary for a person with dementia. As the end of Don's life neared, I realized it was no longer a kindness to do some of the things that used to give him joy.

Were I again to help someone through dementia, I would tell more gentle lies and let the inaccuracies stand. That may sound strange, but really, what is there to gain by correcting someone whose world is untenable? The important thing is to make them feel secure and let them know they are loved.

One of the challenges of being around a person with dementia is listening to the same statement or question repeated over and over. There is absolutely no good in pointing out that they just told you or asked you that. Our driveway is not very long, and to keep myself from screaming, I used to count the number of times Don would ask where we were going before we reached the street. It became something of a game, to see how many repetitions he could fit into those 30 seconds. Once on the open road, the questions slowed down, probably because there were welcome distractions.

If dementia is hard for us adults to comprehend,

imagine how difficult it must be for young children to understand why grandpa is acting erratically. For this reason, we did not usually babysit our granddaughter. However, one day, when she was three, both her parents needed to work nearby, so they decided to risk entrusting her to us. Don was, at the time, into his Terrible Twos.

As we were returning her to her folks, I heard from the back seat, "Grandpa Don sure does say 'no' a lot."

"Yes," I said cheerfully. "It's his favorite word." I added, "Was there a time when you used to say 'no' a lot?"

Silence. And then her small voice responded, "Yes."

Don's daughter and her husband eventually found a good way to describe to our granddaughter what was going on with Don. This was Important Information for an almost-four-year-old. By then, Don was in foster care, and when I brought her to visit him, she proudly explained to one and all that, "Grandpa Don has an owie in his brain." She was toying with the pieces of a jigsaw puzzle on the table, as she announced it several times to the general airwaves. Then she added a couple more times to one of the other residents, who was seated nearby. And finally, she said it directly to Don. "Grandpa Don, you have an owie in your brain."

"Yes," I told her. "I think he knows it." But at least now she had an explanation for his unpredictable behavior, and she could experience it without it diminishing their love for each other.

About the time Don's father was nearing the end of his life, at age 100, I went to a caregivers presentation. I asked what I should say to Don when his dad died and was told to explain it gently one time, but just once. Beyond that, to tell someone of the death of a loved one only makes them go through grief afresh. Because his father lived in another state, the subject didn't come up as it might have had Don been used to seeing him on a regular basis. Otherwise, I would've had to invent reasons for his absence—a trip, an arrival later in the day, a scheduling conflict.

Several of my fellow caregivers told of creative responses they'd come up with, in a variety of circumstances, to play along with an altered Universe. Some of them were full of humor. One normally mild-mannered man told of cursing in exasperation at his wife. Later, she told him about a "mean man" who'd been in the house. "You let me know if you see him again," the husband said valiantly. "I'll take care of him!" We might as well have fun, while we're keeping others happy. When dealing with dementia, The Truth can be highly overrated.

In the vein of soothing fears, Charlie Brown's friend, Linus, was not the only one

Grandpa/Granddaughter
Adoration Society

in need of a security blanket. As I have related before, taking Don to medical appointments was a real struggle for both of us. Toward the end, Don latched onto a very personal talisman. For his 70th birthday, a dear friend had asked me to send her some of Don's poems. She combined them into a beautiful book, with photos, including one of Don, Bear, Misty, and me on the back cover. Don had taken the book to a dental appointment, and it seemed to give him great comfort. So the day he had to go to the ER in an ambulance, I made sure he had the book clutched in his hand, while I followed behind in the car. To see his name printed on the front of the book and our picture on the back kept his sense of identity intact in the midst of unfamiliar surroundings.

Getting a card in the mail had a similar effect on Don's self-identity. I would walk into his room and find him clutching the envelope from a birthday card, pointing to his name and saying it out loud. This was who he was, and that writing proved it! We might want to remember this when friends end up in memory care. They do not want to be forgotten, perhaps especially to themselves.

It was interesting to realize, though it shouldn't have surprised me, that Don didn't connect with photographs from his younger years. But pictures of him that looked more like the man in the mirror, with a story about where it was taken and what we were doing, brought a smile of recognition.

I first tumbled to this form of entertainment when

we celebrated our 25th wedding anniversary, shortly after I put him in foster care. In an effort to salvage the day (mostly for myself, since calendar dates had long ceased to matter to Don), I grabbed several packets of wedding photos. We'd had a "no presents" wedding but asked people who enjoyed taking pictures to be our photographers. Thus, we had numerous envelopes to look through, and over the course of several days, we did just that. From then on, we strolled often down Memory Lane. I had a drawer full of photos of our life together, which gave us both many hours of enjoyment.

I also found it made Don happy when I brought short videos of friends sending their greetings. With today's technology, it's such an easy thing to do, and I'm sure it made him feel he was still loved. When there wasn't time to get a video, even a quick snapshot gave him another friend with whom to reconnect. And, as I have mentioned before, in-person visits worked well when I was there to help keep the conversation going. Friends are usually more comfortable if they are not the only ones in the room trying to talk to someone who is basically non-verbal, and my presence also meant Don did not feel he had to keep people entertained single-handedly. In fact, he seemed just as happy to simply listen in on our conversations. It was a sense of connection, with no obligation on his part.

The first time Don celebrated his birthday in the foster care home, I realized I had misjudged his ability to be around a larger group of friends. To honor his

75th, I decided to host an open house in the care home's communal living room. I specified a window of two hours, in the hope people would drop in at different times. But in the end, we had eight or ten of us in the room at once.

Don was in Heaven! All those people were there to see HIM and love on HIM. And yes, there was dessert. Two kinds, to be precise.

Fortunately, at the last minute I had a Brilliant Idea: name tags! This absolved my husband of wracking his brain for his visitors' identities. It proved an easy way to circumvent unwanted anxiety, and since the package came with 100 name tags, I continued to use them, even with close family.

As a musician, I would be remiss if I did not mention the potency of this art form to stimulate memories. Apparently, music lights up more parts of the brain than almost anything else. People who are non-verbal can still sing the lyrics to songs they loved decades earlier. This left me searching for something we could share, but when I came up empty-handed, I realized it was mostly classical instrumental music that had been our milieu. No words needed. So I played Bach for him, and we were both comforted.

I did, however, make a happy discovery while Don was still living at home. Although many other live performances became too hard for him to focus on, ballet proved to be perfect for him. There were vivid colors and action and beautiful music, and these held his attention, even if he didn't understand the plot. I highly recommend this art form.

If you are caring for someone with dementia, you don't need me to tell you how hard it can be. Most of us come to it with little or no training, groping our way as we go. There will likely be times you feel you're doing a terrible job, that the task is overwhelming, unrelenting, and impossible.

Please, please, please, accept help from others. I've watched too many people try to go it alone for far longer than was healthy for anyone involved. Find a support group. They are such a source of collective wisdom, understanding, and outright laughter. No one will comprehend better what you're going through than your fellow caregivers.

Friends helped me greatly along the way. One of the best presents I ever received was a coupon from a friend for two hours a week visiting Don. She offered it out of her already very busy schedule, which made it all the more touching. Unfortunately, at that stage in Don's decline, he was too fearful for it to work for him, but it didn't detract one bit from my appreciation of the gift.

I don't know if people who extended words of encouragement had any idea how much it meant to me. To be in church and have someone tell me they admired the care I was giving Don set me up to face another week. One friend even said watching us together was a deep spiritual experience for her. Please, do not cut yourself off from this sustenance. As much as Don needed to stay connected, so did I.

And finally, be good to yourself. Adjust your standards to the ever-changing reality. Remember the airline's instructions to put on your own oxygen mask first. You do not want to add to the statistics of caregivers who predecease the people they are tending. Find humor wherever possible. It's a bizarre journey, so you might as well laugh.

Do what you can, with whatever love you can manage under the circumstances. In the end, it's all anyone can ask of you.

Afterward

Small Triumphs

As I write this, it is now more than a year since Don died. Looking back on almost a decade of dealing with his dementia, I am surprised at how fertile that time was. Every day brought new challenges and more "adventures." Bit by bit, extraneous things fell away, and we were left with our essence. It was probably the hardest season of my life, but it was not without its rewards.

With Alzheimer's, Don lost both his short-term and long-term memory. Which put us very much in the moment. He had always been better than I at observing little pleasures on our walks. His disease forced me to slow down and see the world through his childlike perception. In "normal" life, there is often not much occasion to remark about mundane minutiae, but they enrich our souls in meaningful ways. We need only take the time to notice.

This book is sprinkled with small triumphs I encountered as we dealt with the dementia—moments of humor or poignancy or beauty. Victories, when the person I was losing resurfaced, however briefly. Two simple words, as Don's face lit up in recognition one day: "You're mine!"

Perhaps my greatest gift from this encounter with Alzheimer's is a profound sense of gratitude. Sounds improbable, doesn't it? But all along the way, I had glimpses of how bad it could get and knew that somehow we were being spared the worst. When you look into the abyss, the ground under your feet becomes extremely precious.

Don is still very much with me. I greet each day in the bedroom we were refurbishing at the beginning of this book. My futon is oriented in a different direction from how our bed used to be, in part for better use of the space and, at some level, to allow my life to go in a new direction. I open my eyes to the bright yellow walls and light blue ceiling we painted together— colors we chose so that, no matter what the weather, we could wake each morning to sunshine and blue skies.

I got a new iPhone recently. As I was trying to figure out how to make it work, I swiped right and suddenly, there was a picture of Don—a photo I had forgotten about but taken three years earlier, just before he moved into foster care. He is standing in front of his beloved camellia bush, which is laden with red blossoms...and he is waving at me.

Coincidence? Or perhaps one more small triumph.

CAMELLIA

Three years ago
You asked me the name.
"Camellia," I said.
You smiled, and a few minutes later
Asked again.
"Camellia."
You nodded.
Eventually, you wrote it down
But still asked.

Two years ago
It was in full riot
Turning our dining room window
Into an ecstasy
Of red blossoms.
You pointed.
What is the name?
"Camellia," I said.
You wrote it down
But still you asked.

Last year
There were not so many blossoms
As if the bush were
Disheartened by your absence.
But I picked a few of its flowers

And your face lit up in recognition
When I brought them to you.

This year
It will bloom for me alone
And I will ache to tell you again,
"Camellia."

Camellias from a friend

Homecoming, Celebration, and Laughter

I t is now September of 2022. Don has been gone for more than 2 1/2 years. And yet, he can still make me laugh.

I want to share two events that happened earlier this year.

The first began on Valentine's Day, when I got a letter from Oregon Health & Science University, saying Don's remains were now ready to be sent to me. They were done using him for research and education. It was decidedly the strangest valentine I'd ever received, but then, we loved quirky humor.

At that point, I was in the midst of a major plumbing project, complete with an army of plumbers and an eye-popping bill, all of which I found fairly draining (bad, but accurate, pun). Finally, on the afternoon of February 24th, the last of the plumbers went out the back door.

About 15 minutes later, there was a knock at the front door. There stood the mail carrier, in need of my signature for Don's remains. As I took the box, I was filled with conflicting emotions. Holding my husband's ashes, the grim reality of my loss confronted me. How could so much life be reduced to something so small and mundane? And really, I was already worn out by the invasion of the plumbers. Couldn't this wait for another day?

And then I began to laugh.

Don so detested doing plumbing work that we had a joke. He used to say (though it was not true) that when he met me, he introduced himself as, "Hi, I'm Don. I don't do plumbing."

Obviously, he had waited until it was safe to come home.

The second event happened a few months later. After three unsuccessful tries, we were finally able to have a hybrid Celebration of Life for Don! My entire nuclear family (all six of them) flew up from Los Angeles for the event. Don's daughter and her family, as well as his younger sister and her husband, were also there. As were friends, many of whom had never met Don. Zoom allowed others, near and far, to join us online.

I was immeasurably touched that the people who had agreed to be part of the service—the minister, the chamber choir and conductor, the pianist and organist —had stuck with me through all the rescheduling. And it could not have landed on a more perfect date, May 1st.

May Day was already full of meaning, with its promise of flowers and bright colors, both of which Don loved. But a few days prior to the service, I became aware that May 1st was also World Laughter Day. What more could I ask for to honor the man who made us laugh?!

The long delay had also been a blessing. It allowed me time to resurrect a more complete portrait of the man who had slowly disappeared from our lives. It also gave me time to transmute the grief of his loss into a celebration of the man we all loved.

I discovered poetry he'd written before I knew him and had a couple of them read during the service. Spurred on by World Laughter Day, people told funny Don stories. The tributes and the music brought tears to my eyes. I played the Prelude to Bach's first cello suite on my viola, as my love letter to him.

And then there were the camellia blossoms! The tree Don had cherished had never been so full of buds as it was this year. I thought wistfully about how beautiful it would be to have them at the service. But camellia flowers rarely last beyond a few weeks, and the tree started blooming in mid-March. Then we had an unusually cool, wet spring, and on May 1st I had no problem cutting a dozen beautiful red camellia blossoms, one for each family member to contribute to a special bouquet as we walked into the sanctuary.

Small triumphs come in many forms. Perhaps the best one of all is being able to recognize them when they bless us.

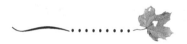

ACKNOWLEDGMENTS

So many people have contributed to this book—a word here, a thought there, sometimes whole concepts to consider—that I fear I will miss recognizing someone. If I do, and this is you, I apologize in advance. The past three years, marked by COVID and grieving, as well as the joy of writing and emerging into a new life, have given me plenty of things to keep track of. In short, I should have kept a list of all your kindnesses.

That being said, I will begin with the group that first heard this book, as I read it chapter by chapter in Pat Arnold's writing class. You were there at the beginning, encouraging me to keep at it, asking pertinent questions, reminding me it was a worthy endeavor. You were the team that cheered me on, week after week, as Don used to do when he was alive. I am more grateful than you can imagine. Thank you, also, Pat, for the time you spent giving me extra feedback. You went above and beyond, with your usual generosity of spirit.

To my friends and fellow writers who agreed to read the book in one of its many incarnations, you each made an impact on the final product: Betsy Parker, BJ Novitski, Bobbi Parker, David Frackelton, Elizabeth Lorish, Ellen Stern, Elli Hall, Janet Johnson, MJ Williams, Naomi Wamacks, Ted Stern. My deepest thanks.

When Paul Iarrobino was putting together an

anthology about how we had coped with COVID, I reworked the chapter "Grieving During a Pandemic," and received valuable editorial comments from both him and Sittrea Friberg, for which I am extremely grateful. It was an honor to participate in the creation of *COVIDOLOGY: Sharing Life Lessons from Behind the Mask.*

After I had taken the book as far as I could within my circle of friends and colleagues, I went in search of a professional editor who didn't know us but knew the business. Kim Griswell, you have been a godsend. Your suggestions have been "spot on" and have made this book worlds better than it would have been without you. Knowing that you are a fellow musician was already a bonus, but imagine my joy at discovering you are also skilled in book design! May this be the first of many collaborations.

And finally, Don, if you're looking over my shoulder reading this, thank you for an amazing life together. To paraphrase Mr. Rogers, you are the person who most "loved me into being." I am forever blessed.

ABOUT THE AUTHOR

Holly Stern is a native Oregonian who has made her career as a classical violinist, playing with both modern and period instrument ensembles. Writing has been a lifelong passion of hers, and she's bursting at the seams to have finally written her first book. Next to be published will be a compilation of humorous cat stories, *Theo's Cat-a-Blog: Adventures and Advice from a Young Black Cat*. Holly also enjoys gardening, hiking, biking, and reading good books on the couch with Theo the Cat.

A portion of the profits from this book will be donated to the Alzheimer's Association.

Made in the USA
Middletown, DE
22 November 2023

43276423R00076